Just Research

Aspen Coursebook Series

Just Research
Preparing for Practice

Fourth Edition

Laurel Currie Oates
Professor of Law
Seattle University School of Law

Anne Enquist
Professor of Lawyering Skills
Director, Legal Writing Program
Seattle University School of Law

Wolters Kluwer
Law & Business

Published by Wolters Kluwer Law & Business in New York.

Wolters Kluwer Law & Business serves customers worldwide with CCH, Aspen Publishers, and Kluwer Law International products. (www.wolterskluwerlb.com)

To contact Customer Service, e-mail customer.service@wolterskluwer.com, call 1-800-234-1660, fax 1-800-901-9075, or mail correspondence to:

Wolters Kluwer Law & Business
Attn: Order Department
PO Box 990
Frederick, MD 21705

Printed in the United States of America.

1 2 3 4 5 6 7 8 9 0

ISBN 978-1-4548-3100-6

Library of Congress Cataloging-in-Publication Data

Oates, Laurel Currie, 1951- author.
  Just research / Laurel Currie Oates, Professor of Law, Director, Legal Writing Program, Seattle University School of Law, Anne Enquist, Professor of Lawyering Skills, Associate Director, Legal Writing Program, Seattle University School of Law. -- Fourth edition.
    p. cm. -- (Aspen coursebook series)
  ISBN 978-1-4548-3100-6
  1. Legal research--United States. I. Enquist, Anne, 1950- author. II. Title.
KF240.O18 2014
340.072'073--dc23
                                                              2013039768

About Wolters Kluwer Law & Business

Wolters Kluwer Law & Business is a leading global provider of intelligent information and digital solutions for legal and business professionals in key specialty areas, and respected educational resources for professors and law students. Wolters Kluwer Law & Business connects legal and business professionals as well as those in the education market with timely, specialized authoritative content and information-enabled solutions to support success through productivity, accuracy and mobility.

Serving customers worldwide, Wolters Kluwer Law & Business products include those under the Aspen Publishers, CCH, Kluwer Law International, Loislaw, ftwilliam.com and MediRegs family of products.

CCH products have been a trusted resource since 1913, and are highly regarded resources for legal, securities, antitrust and trade regulation, government contracting, banking, pension, payroll, employment and labor, and healthcare reimbursement and compliance professionals.

Aspen Publishers products provide essential information to attorneys, business professionals and law students. Written by preeminent authorities, the product line offers analytical and practical information in a range of specialty practice areas from securities law and intellectual property to mergers and acquisitions and pension/benefits. Aspen's trusted legal education resources provide professors and students with high-quality, up-to-date and effective resources for successful instruction and study in all areas of the law.

Kluwer Law International products provide the global business community with reliable international legal information in English. Legal practitioners, corporate counsel and business executives around the world rely on Kluwer Law journals, looseleafs, books, and electronic products for comprehensive information in many areas of international legal practice.

Loislaw is a comprehensive online legal research product providing legal content to law firm practitioners of various specializations. Loislaw provides attorneys with the ability to quickly and efficiently find the necessary legal information they need, when and where they need it, by facilitating access to primary law as well as state-specific law, records, forms and treatises.

ftwilliam.com offers employee benefits professionals the highest quality plan documents (retirement, welfare and non-qualified) and government forms (5500/PBGC, 1099 and IRS) software at highly competitive prices.

MediRegs products provide integrated health care compliance content and software solutions for professionals in healthcare, higher education and life sciences, including professionals in accounting, law and consulting.

Wolters Kluwer Law & Business, a division of Wolters Kluwer, is headquartered in New York. Wolters Kluwer is a market-leading global information services company focused on professionals.

Dedication

We dedicate this book to our students,
who keep us looking toward the future.

Laurel Currie Oates
Anne Enquist

Summary of Contents

Contents

List of Materials in the Electronic Supplement

See http://www.aspenlawschool.com/books/oates_legalwritinghandbook/.

Chapter 4: Researching Issues Governed by State Statutes

Chapter 5: Researching Issues Governed by Federal Statutes

Preface

About eight years ago, we had one of those "ah ha" moments. In a single instant, we knew, not how to make a better mouse trap, but how to write a better legal research book.

A. A Short History of Legal Research Books

The first generation of legal research books described the sources available to legal researchers. Each chapter focused on a particular source (for example, codes, digests, or reporters), detailing the source and how it was updated. Although these books were a treasure chest of useful information, they did not discuss the process of researching a problem. Thus, after reading these books, a beginning researcher knew what the sources were but not how to use them.

The second generation of legal research books tried to remedy this problem by describing not only the sources but the process of researching a legal issue. Unfortunately, though, most of these books used the same organizational scheme that was used in the first generation of books. Although the books talked, in general terms, about the process of researching a problem, each chapter focused on a particular source. In addition, although this second generation of books talked about electronic sources, the focus was on doing legal research using books. In most of the textbooks, each chapter started with a discussion of the books and ended with a brief description of fee-based services like LexisNexis® and Westlaw.

B. How *Just Research* Differs from Existing Legal Research Books

Just Research begins a new generation of books about legal research: It breaks with tradition in three ways. First, *Just Research* is organized around issues rather than sources; second, *Just Research* emphasizes the use of free and fee-based electronic sources; and third, like most legal sources, *Just Research* is available both as a book and as an e-book.

1. Issues vs. Sources

Because lawyers research issues, we have organized *Just Research* around those issues rather than sources. As a consequence, instead of describing a particular source, each chapter describes how to research a particular type of issue. For example, Chapter 4 describes the sources and process that is used in researching an issue that is governed by a state statute, Chapter 5 describes the sources and process that is used in researching an issue that is governed by federal statutes and regulations, Chapter 6 describes the sources and process of researching an issue governed by local ordinances, and so on.

2. Electronic Sources vs. Books; Fee-based vs. Free

Until a few years ago, few people viewed computers neutrally. Computers were either high-tech demons that depersonalized and dehumanized modern life, or they were the solution to all problems. The same was true of computer-assisted research. Attorneys saw computer-assisted research either as an overrated, overpriced shortcut that produced poor results or as the most efficient and reliable means of accessing information. Although there are a few people who still oppose computer-assisted research, most attorneys now prefer electronic research to book research, with many attorneys doing their research almost exclusively online.

The more recent legal research controversy concerns fee-based sources vs. free sources. Initially many of us were skeptical about the free sources and worried about relying on them. In some cases the skepticism was justified, but as with so many other things with the Internet, over time people have come to learn what is and is not reliable information. As a result, in many instances, free government and educational websites have become the source of choice. Accordingly, the electronic supplement and e-book show you how to do research using not only fee-based services but also free sources.

3. Book vs. E-book

For the first time, *Just Research* is available as both a book and as an e-book. If you have purchased the book, use the book to find general information about researching different types of legal issues, and then go to the website (the URL and your password are on a card in the front of the book) to see how to use that general information to research specific issues using free sources, Lexis Advance®, WestlawNext™, Bloomberg Law, Lexis.com®, and Westlaw® Classic. If you have purchased the e-book, everything that you need is in the e-book. While we do not expect that everyone will read all of the "how to" sections, we urge you to read several comparing and contrasting the fee-based services and learning what types of information are available for free. While we do not recommend that you do all of your research using free sources, sites like Google™ Scholar can be an excellent starting point and can lower your research costs.

4. A Final Comment

A book that focuses on electronic sources presents a special challenge: Those sources keep changing. It seems that as soon as we capture a screen from free sources, Lexis Advance®, WestlawNext™, Bloomberg Law, Lexis.com®, and Westlaw® Classic, something changes. Thus, although we will update the screen shots in the e-book on a regular basis, the examples that you see in the electronic supplement or e-book may not match what you see on your own computer screen. We are confident, however, that these changes will not present too much confusion for our readers because, as we have emphasized throughout *Just Research*, the key to becoming an excellent legal researcher is knowledge of the underlying structure, not the surface features.

Acknowledgments

Although some people believe that writing is a solitary process, this book disproves that belief. The process of writing this book has allowed us to engage in wonderful conversations with our colleagues and students about how the process of researching legal issues has changed during the last ten years and about the best ways of preparing students for the future.

We would like to begin by thanking our students and alumni. Thank you for sharing with us your experiences as summer associates, legal interns, legal externs, and practicing attorneys. Your insights into how technology is changing legal research have been invaluable

We would also like to the people who helped us with this book. First, we would like to thank Matthew Enquist for giving up his valuable time to create the exquisite drawings that appear in Chapter 1. Thank you so much. Second, we would like to thank Professor Mimi Samuel for providing both technical and moral support and Aaron Meyers, our Lexis representative, for his help in updating the sections on LexisNexis® and for teaching us how to use Lexis® Advance. Third, we would like to thank our current research assistants, Ahmad Khalaf and Lorie Hahn. We know that capturing screen shots and updating exercises is not the most glamorous work. Our biggest thanks, however, go to the people at Aspen who helped us with this project. Our deepest thanks go to Dana Wilson for helping us with this project and all of our other projects. We have thoroughly enjoyed working with you. In addition, thanks to Lisa Wehrle, who worked on the manuscript, to Enid Zafran who prepared the index, to Sharon Ray who did the composition, and to Karen Quigley for her cover design.

Last, but certainly not least, we would like to thank our families. Laurel sends her love to her husband, Terry, and her children, Julia and Michael, and the important people in their lives, big Michael and little Michelle. Anne is grateful to her husband Steve for his unfailing love and support, and to her sons and their wives, Matt and Mary and Jeff and Ilana, for their continued love and encouragement.

Just Research

Introduction to Legal Research

Fortresses, Tumors, and Legal Research

§ 1.1   Two Puzzles

We begin this book with two puzzles. While neither presents a legal question, together they demonstrate an important point about legal research.

> Pretend for a moment that it is the year 1900 and that you are a general who has been sent to free a small country that has fallen under the rule of a ruthless dictator. This dictator rules his country from a fortress that can be reached by a number of roads radiating outward like spokes on a wheel.
>
> You have been given a great army and are preparing to lead your soldiers into battle when one of your spies brings you a disturbing report. According to this spy, the dictator has planted mines on each of the roads leading to the fortress. Although these mines have been set so that small groups of the dictator's subjects can pass over them safely, any large force would detonate the mines. Not only would this blow up the road and render it impassable, but the dictator would then destroy many villages in retaliation. Therefore, a full-scale direct attack on the fortress is impossible.[1]

What do you do?

After thinking through your options, you come up with a brilliant strategy.

---

1. Adapted from Mary L. Gick & Keith J. Holyoak, *Analogical Problem Solving*, 12 Cognitive Psychology 306, 349 (1980).

Graphic design by Matthew Enquist

Instead of sending all your soldiers to the fort via one road, you divide your army into groups and dispatch each group to the head of a different road. When everyone is in place, you give the signal, and each group charges down a different road toward the fortress. All the small groups pass safely over the mines, and then the army attacks the fortress in full strength. In this way, you are able to capture the fortress and overthrow the dictator.[2]

Now try the following puzzle.

It is now 1950, and you are a doctor with a patient who has a malignant tumor in her stomach. It is impossible to operate on the patient, but unless the tumor is destroyed the patient will die. Fortunately, there is a kind of "ray" that can be used to destroy the tumor. If the rays reach the tumor all at once at a sufficiently high intensity, the tumor will be destroyed. Unfortunately, however, at this intensity, the healthy tissue that the rays pass through on the way to the tumor will also be destroyed. At lower intensities the rays are harmless to healthy tissue, but they do not affect the tumor either. What type of procedure might be used to destroy the tumor with the rays and at the same time avoid destroying the healthy tissue?[3]

---

2. *Id.* at 351.

3. *Id.*

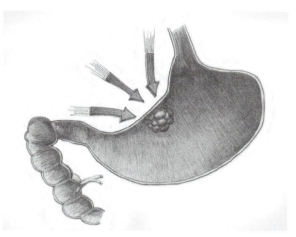

Graphic design by Matthew Enquist

On a first read, these two problems may appear to have nothing in common. The first one takes place in 1900 and involves a general attacking a fortress; the second one takes place in 1950 and involves a doctor trying to destroy a tumor. Upon closer inspection, however, the problems have some interesting parallels: In both problems there is an object that must be destroyed; in both problems a direct attack will not work; and in both problems the solution requires division and then convergence. The "force" must be divided, and the object attacked simultaneously from several different directions. While the "surface features" or facts of these two problems are different, their underlying structures are the same.

So what does all of this have to do with legal research? A common mistake that many researchers make is that they focus on the surface features of the problems and not their underlying structures. For example, when asked to research a problem, they tend to think of the issue in terms of the subject matter: the Family and Medical Leave Act, adverse possession, the Fourth Amendment. Because each of these issues involves a different subject matter, the tendency is to think of them as entirely different problems. Thus, instead of using a proven problem-solving strategy, many researchers reinvent the wheel. Instead of building on what they learned researching and solving other legal problems, they start from scratch.

This research book is designed to help you see the underlying structures. The goal is to show you the structures and then show you how you can use these structures to research a variety of different problems.

§ 1.2   Two Approaches to Learning How to Do Legal Research

There is, of course, more than one way to learn how to solve a particular set of puzzles or problems. The most common way is through trial and error.

Given enough variations of the fortress and tumor problems, you would begin to see the underlying structure and start looking for it.

It is this "discovery" method that underlies the teaching strategy that is used in most law school classrooms. After reading enough cases, you will begin to see that most judicial opinions have the same underlying structure. Most judges begin their opinions by setting out the procedural history and facts. They then go through the issues raised on appeal one at a time, setting out the rules, discussing other cases that are on point, and setting out their holding and reasoning.

In addition, after reading enough cases involving a particular area of law, you will begin to see how that area of law is structured. For instance, after reading enough torts cases, you will begin to realize that all torts fall into one of three categories: intentional torts, negligence, or strict liability. Similarly, after reading enough negligence cases, you will begin to understand that the first question is always whether there was a duty; the second question is always whether there was a breach of that duty; the third question is always whether the breach caused the harm; and the last question always relates to the nature of the damages.

While you tend to remember best the things that you "discover" on your own, the discovery process is time consuming. For most people, for example, discovering the structures underlying legal analysis and, therefore, learning to think like a lawyer, takes at least the three years that they are in law school. Similarly, to learn the structures underlying legal research, you would need to research 10, 20, 30, or even 100 different issues.

As a consequence, instead of using the discovery method, we have chosen the approach advocated by the educational psychologists who developed the fortress and tumor problems. Instead of starting with the puzzle or legal issue, we start by describing the underlying structures. We do not, however, stop there. So that you can apply or "transfer" that structure to new issues, we provide you with a number of different examples, each of which involves different facts or surface features.

An example helps to illustrate the difference between the two methods. If we used the discovery method, we would give you the fortress, tumor, and similar problems and let you figure out, on your own, that all these problems had the same underlying structure and, thus, the same solution. In contrast, in this book we teach you to do legal research by describing the most commonly used strategies for researching legal issues and then illustrating how you can use those strategies to research a variety of legal issues.

§ 1.3   The Structures Underlying Legal Research

So, what are the strategies that are most commonly used in researching legal issues? While the fortress and tumor puzzles involved a division and convergence strategy, almost all legal research involves the following four steps:

1. Familiarizing yourself with the area of law;
2. Locating, reading, and analyzing primary authority;

3. Making sure that the primary authority that you have found is good law; and

4. When appropriate, locating additional primary and secondary authorities.

Thus, a generic research plan would look like this.

Generic Research Plan

Step 1:   If you are unfamiliar with the area of law, spend 10 to 60 minutes reading about the area of law in a secondary source.

Step 2:   Locate, read, and analyze the primary authority.

Step 3:   Cite check primary authority to make sure that it is still good law.

Step 4:   If appropriate, locate and read additional primary and secondary authorities.

Although the steps will remain the same, the sources that you will use will differ depending on two factors: the type of law and the "jurisdiction." Therefore, before researching a problem, ask yourself two questions: first, whether the issue is governed by enacted law, common law, constitutional law, or court rules; and, second, whether the issue is governed by federal law, state law, or local law.

> **PRACTICE POINTER**   You will not always know what type of law governs a particular issue or whether a particular issue involves federal, state, or local law. In these situations, ask someone who is more familiar with the area of law (for example, your supervising attorney or a colleague who has more experience) or look for the answer during the first step, when you are familiarizing yourself with the area of law. (Chapter 3 gives you some guidance on how to determine what law governs an issue.)

When you add these two questions, the generic research plan looks like this.

Generic Research Plan

Type of Law: Is this issue governed by enacted law? Common law? A court rule?

Jurisdiction: Is this issue governed by federal law? State law? Local law?

Step 1:   If you are unfamiliar with the area of law, spend 10 to 60 minutes reading about the area of law in a secondary source.

Step 2:   Locate, read, and analyze the primary authority.

Step 3:   Cite check primary authority to make sure that it is still good law.

Step 4:   If appropriate, locate and read additional primary and secondary authorities.

Before doing the research, you also need to decide how you will do that research. Will you do the research using books; using free Internet sites; using fee-based services such as Lexis Advance®, WestlawNext™, or Bloomberg Law; or using a combination of books, free websites, and fee-based services? Because you cannot make this decision without knowing how to use free websites and the fee-based services, this book — and the supplement that accompanies it — discuss all of these options.

The United States Legal System

The United States system of government. For some, it is the secret to democracy, the power to elect one's leaders and the right to speak freely. For others, it is a horrendous bureaucracy, a maze through which one must struggle to obtain a benefit, to change a law, or to get a day in court. For still others, it is more abstract — a chart in an eighth-grade civics book describing the three branches of government and explaining the system of checks and balances.

For lawyers, the United States system of government is all of these things and more. It is the foundation for their knowledge of the law, the stage on which they play out their professional roles, the arena for the very serious game of law.

No matter which metaphor you prefer — foundation, stage, arena — the point is the same. To be an effective researcher, you must understand the system. You must know the framework before you can work well within it.

Like most complex systems, the United States system of government can be analyzed in a number of different ways. You can focus on its three branches — the executive branch, the legislative branch, and the judicial branch — or you can focus on the system's two parts, the federal government and the state governments.

In this chapter we do both. We look first at the three branches, examining both their individual functions and their interrelationships. We then examine the relationship between state and federal government, again with an eye toward their individual functions and powers.

§ 2.1   The Three Branches of Government

Just as the medical student must understand both the various organs that make up the human body and their relationship to each other, the law student must understand both the three branches of government and the relationships among them.

§ 2.1.1   The Executive Branch

The first of the three branches is the executive branch. In the federal system, the executive power is vested in the President; in the states, it is vested in the governor. (See Article II, Section 1 of the United States Constitution and the constitutions of the various states.) In general, the executive branch has the power to implement and enforce laws. It oversees public projects, administers public benefit programs, and controls law enforcement agencies.

The executive branch also has powers that directly affect our system of law. For example, the President (or a governor) can control the law-making function of the legislative branch by exercising his or her power to convene and adjourn the Congress (or state legislature) or by vetoing legislation. Similarly, the President (or a governor) can shape the decisions of the courts through his or her judicial nominations or by directing the attorney general to enforce or not to enforce certain laws.

§ 2.1.2   The Legislative Branch

The second branch is the legislative branch. Congress's powers are enumerated in Article I, Section 8, of the United States Constitution, which gives Congress, among other things, the power to lay and collect taxes, borrow money, regulate commerce with foreign nations and among the states, establish uniform naturalization and bankruptcy laws, promote the progress of science and the useful arts by creating copyright laws, and punish counterfeiting. Powers not granted Congress are given to the states or left to the people. (See the Tenth Amendment to the United States Constitution.) The state constitutions enumerate the powers given to the state legislatures.

Like the executive branch, the legislative branch exercises power over the other two branches. It can check the actions of the executive branch by enacting or refusing to enact legislation requested by the executive, by controlling the budget and, at least at the federal level, by consenting or refusing to consent to nominations made by the executive.

The legislative branch's power over the judicial branch is less obvious. At one level, it can control the judiciary through its power to establish courts (Article I, Section 8, grants Congress the power to establish inferior federal courts) and its power to consent to or reject the executive branch's judicial nominations. However, the most obvious control it has over the judiciary is its power to enact legislation that supersedes, or replaces, a common law or court-made doctrine or rule.

The legislative branch also shares its law-making power with the executive branch. In enacting legislation, it sometimes gives the executive branch the power to promulgate the regulations needed to implement or enforce the legislation. For example, although Congress (the legislative branch) enacted the Internal Revenue Code, the Internal Revenue Service (part of the executive branch) promulgates the regulations needed to implement that code.

§ 2.1.3　The Judicial Branch

The third branch is the judicial branch. Article III, Section 1, of the United States Constitution vests the judicial power of the United States in one supreme court and in such inferior courts as Congress may establish. The state constitutions establish and grant power to the state courts.

a.　The Hierarchical Nature of the Court System

Both the federal and the state court systems are hierarchical. At the lowest level are the trial courts, whose primary function is fact-finding. The judge or jury hears the evidence and enters a judgment.

At the next level are the intermediate courts of appeals. These courts hear the majority of appeals, deciding (1) whether the trial court applied the right law and (2) whether there is sufficient evidence to support the jury's verdict or the trial judge's findings of fact and conclusions of law. Unlike the trial courts, these courts do not conduct trials. There are no witnesses, and the only exhibits are the exhibits that were admitted during trial. The decisions of the appellate courts are based solely on the written record and the attorneys' arguments.

At the top level are the states' highest courts and the Supreme Court of the United States. The primary function of these courts is to make law. They hear only those cases that involve issues of great public import or cases in which different divisions or circuits have adopted or applied conflicting rules of law. Like the intermediate courts of appeals, these courts do not hear evidence; they only review the trial court record. See Chart 2.1.

An example illustrates the role each court plays. In *State v. Strong*, a criminal case, the defendant, Mr. Strong, was charged with possession of a controlled substance. At the trial court level, both the State and the defendant presented witnesses and physical evidence. On the basis of this evidence, the trial court decided the case on its merits, with the trial judge deciding the questions of law (whether the evidence should be suppressed) and the jury deciding the questions of fact (whether the State had proved all of the elements of the crime beyond a reasonable doubt).

Both issues were decided against the defendant: The trial court judge ruled that the evidence was admissible, and the jury found that the State had met its burden of proof. Disagreeing with both determinations, the defendant filed an appeal with the intermediate court of appeals.

In deciding this appeal, the appellate court could consider only two issues: whether the trial court judge erred when he denied the defendant's motion to suppress and whether there was sufficient evidence to support the jury's verdict.

Because the first issue raised a question of law, the appellate court could review the issue de novo. The court did not need to defer to the judgment of the trial court judge. Instead, the appellate court could exercise its own independent judgment to decide the issue on its merits.

The appellate court had much less latitude with respect to the second issue. Because the second issue raised a question of fact rather than law, the appellate court could not substitute its judgment for that of the jury. It could only review the jury's findings to make sure that they were supported by the evidence. When the question is one of fact, the appellate court may decide only (1) whether there is sufficient evidence to support the jury's verdict or (2) whether the jury's verdict is clearly erroneous. It may not substitute its judgment for the judgment of the jury.

Chart 2.1	**The Roles of the Trial, Intermediate, and Supreme Courts**

Trial Court

- The trial court hears witnesses and views evidence.
- The trial court judge decides issues of law; the jury decides questions of fact. (When there is no jury, the trial court judge decides both the questions of law and the questions of fact.)

Intermediate Court of Appeals

- The intermediate court of appeals reviews the written record and exhibits from the trial court.
- When an issue raises a question of law, the intermediate court of appeals may substitute its judgment for the judgment of the trial court judge; when an issue raises a question of fact, the appellate court must defer to the decision of the finder of fact (the jury or, if there was no jury, the trial judge).

Supreme, or Highest, Court

- Like the intermediate court of appeals, it reviews the written record and exhibits from the trial court.
- Like the intermediate court of appeals, it has broad powers to review questions of law: It determines whether the trial court and intermediate court of appeals applied the right law correctly. Its power to review factual issues is, however, very limited. Like the intermediate court of appeals, it can determine only whether there is sufficient evidence to support the decision of the jury or, if there was no jury, the decision of the trial court judge.

Regardless of the type of issue (fact or law), the appellate court must base its decision on the written trial court record and exhibits and the attorneys' arguments. Consequently, in *Strong*, the intermediate court of appeals did not see or hear any of the witnesses. The only people present when the appeal was argued were the appellate court judges assigned to hear the case and Strong's and the State's attorneys. Not even the defendant, Mr. Strong, was present.

If Mr. Strong lost his first appeal, he could petition the state supreme court (through a petition for discretionary review) and ask that court to review the intermediate court of appeals' decision. If the state supreme court granted the petition, its review, like that of the intermediate court of appeals, would be limited. Although the supreme court would review the issue of law de novo, it would have to defer to the jury's decision on the questions of fact.

Most of the cases that appear in law school casebooks are appellate court decisions, for example, decisions of the United States Court of Appeals or the United States Supreme Court or decisions from state appellate courts. These cases, however, represent only a small, and perhaps not representative, percentage of the disputes that lawyers see during the course of their practice.

Accordingly, as you read the cases in the casebooks, remember that you are seeing only the proverbial tip of the iceberg. For a case to reach the United States Supreme Court, the parties must have had the financial means to pursue it, and the Court must have found that the issue raised was significant enough to grant review.

> **PRACTICE POINTER**
>
> As you will learn in Civil Procedure, to hear a case a court must have both subject matter jurisdiction and personal jurisdiction. Stated very simply, a court has subject matter jurisdiction when it has power to hear a particular type of case. For example, the federal courts have subject matter jurisdiction to hear cases involving the United States Constitution and United States statutes, state courts of general jurisdiction have subject matter jurisdiction to hear cases involving the state constitution and state statutes, and municipal courts have subject matter jurisdiction to hear cases involving city ordinances. It is not, though, enough that a court has subject matter jurisdiction. The court must also have personal jurisdiction or the power to hear and decide cases involving the parties to the case or controversy.

b.   The Federal Courts

In the federal system, most cases are heard initially in the federal district courts, the primary trial courts in that system. These courts have original jurisdiction over most federal questions and have the power to review the decisions of some administrative agencies. Each state has at least one district court, and many have several. For example, Indiana has the District Court for Northern Indiana and the District Court for Southern Indiana. Cases that are not heard in the district court are usually heard in one of several specialized courts, for example, the United States Tax Court, the United States Court of Federal Claims, or the United States Court of International Trade.

In the federal system, the intermediate court of appeals is the United States Court of Appeals. There are currently thirteen circuits: eleven numbered circuits, the District of Columbia Circuit, and the Federal Circuit. See Chart 2.2. The Federal Circuit, which was created in 1982, reviews the decisions of the United States Court of Federal Claims and the United States Court of International Trade, as well as some administrative decisions.

> **PRACTICE POINTER**
>
> For an electronic copy of a map showing the federal circuits, see *http://www.uscourts.gov/court_locator.aspx*

| Chart 2.2 | The Thirteen Federal Judicial Circuits |

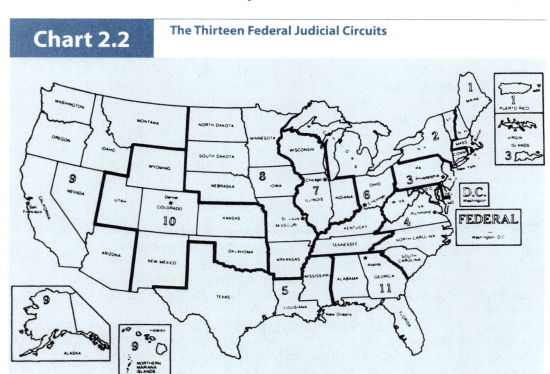

Reprinted from *Federal Reporter* (West's National Reporter System) with permission of West, a Thomson Reuters business.

The highest federal court is the United States Supreme Court. Although many people believe that the Supreme Court is all-powerful, in fact it is not. As with other courts, there are limits on the Supreme Court's powers. It can play only one of two roles.

In one role, the United States Supreme Court is similar to the state supreme courts. In the federal system, the United States Supreme Court is the highest court, the court of last resort. In contrast, in its other role, it is the final arbiter of federal constitutional law, interpreting the United States Constitution and determining whether the federal government or a state has violated rights granted under the United States Constitution.

Thus, although people often assert that they will take their case all the way to the Supreme Court, they may not be able to. As a general rule, the Supreme Court may hear a case only if it involves a question of federal constitutional law or a federal statute. The Supreme Court does not have the power to hear cases involving only questions of state law. For example, although the United States Supreme Court has the power to determine whether a state's marriage dissolution statutes are constitutional, the Court does not have the power to hear purely factual questions, such as whether it would be in the best interests of a child for custody to be granted to the father or whether child support should be set at $300 rather than $400 per month.

Each year the United States Supreme Court receives more than 7,000 requests for review (writs of certiorari). Of the approximately 100 cases that the Court actually hears, the overwhelming majority are appeals from the federal courts.

Chart 2.3 illustrates the relationships among the various federal courts.

Because the United States District Courts and Courts of Appeals hear so many cases, not all of their decisions are "published." When they are published, decisions from the United States District Courts are published in either the *Federal Supplement*, or *Federal Rules Decisions*, and decisions from the United States Courts of Appeals are published in the *Federal Reporter*. (Decisions from the specialized courts are published in specialized reporters.

PRACTICE POINTER	A "published" decision is a decision that is published in a set of books called a "reporter." (For more about reporters, see §4.2.4b.) Thus, decisions that appear on Lexis Advance®, WestlawNext™,

Bloomberg Law, or a free website but that are not in a reporter are not published decisions. They are unpublished, or unreported, decisions. In some jurisdictions, you cannot cite to an unpublished decision in a brief to that jurisdiction's courts. To find out whether you can cite to an unpublished decision, see your local court rules.

All United States Supreme Court decisions are published. The official reporter is *United States Reports*, and the two unofficial reporters are *Supreme Court Reporter* and *United States Supreme Court Reports, Lawyers' Edition*.

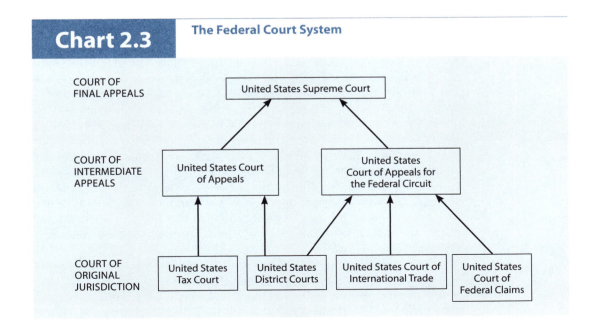

Chart 2.3   **The Federal Court System**

COURT OF FINAL APPEALS — United States Supreme Court

COURT OF INTERMEDIATE APPEALS — United States Court of Appeals / United States Court of Appeals for the Federal Circuit

COURT OF ORIGINAL JURISDICTION — United States Tax Court / United States District Courts / United States Court of International Trade / United States Court of Federal Claims

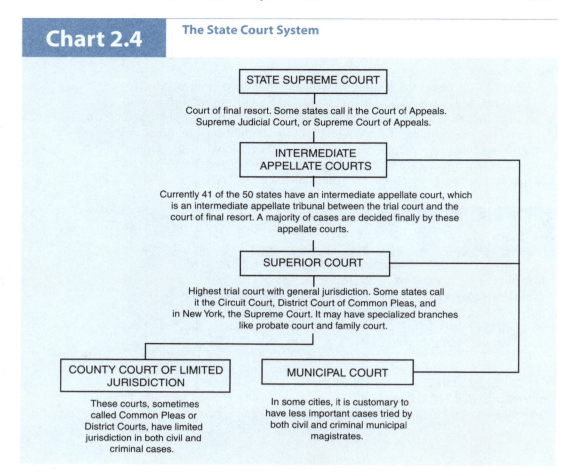

Chart 2.4   **The State Court System**

STATE SUPREME COURT

Court of final resort. Some states call it the Court of Appeals.
Supreme Judicial Court, or Supreme Court of Appeals.

INTERMEDIATE
APPELLATE COURTS

Currently 41 of the 50 states have an intermediate appellate court, which
is an intermediate appellate tribunal between the trial court and the
court of final resort. A majority of cases are decided finally by these
appellate courts.

SUPERIOR COURT

Highest trial court with general jurisdiction. Some states call
it the Circuit Court, District Court of Common Pleas, and
in New York, the Supreme Court. It may have specialized branches
like probate court and family court.

COUNTY COURT OF LIMITED
JURISDICTION

These courts, sometimes
called Common Pleas or
District Courts, have limited
jurisdiction in both civil and
criminal cases.

MUNICIPAL COURT

In some cities, it is customary to
have less important cases tried by
both civil and criminal municipal
magistrates.

c.   State Courts

A number of courts operate within the states. At the lowest level are courts of limited jurisdiction. These courts hear only certain types of cases or cases involving only limited amounts of money. Municipal or city courts are courts of limited jurisdiction, as are county or district courts and small claims courts.

At the next level are courts of general jurisdiction. These courts have the power to review the decisions of courts of limited jurisdiction and original jurisdiction over claims arising under state law, whether that law is the state constitution, state statutes, or state common law.

About three-quarters of the states now have an intermediate court of appeals. These courts hear appeals as of right from the state courts of general jurisdiction, and the bulk of their caseload is criminal appeals. Because of the size of their workload, many of these courts have several divisions or districts.

Every state has a state "supreme" court. These courts review the decisions of the state trial courts and courts of appeals and are the final arbiters of questions of state constitutional, statutory, and common law. Chart 2.4 illustrates the typical relationship among the various state courts.

<table>
<tr><td>**PRACTICE POINTER**</td><td>Not all states call their highest court the supreme court. For example, in New York, the highest court is called the Court of Appeals, and the trial courts are called the supreme courts.</td></tr>
</table>

Decisions of state trial courts are not usually published. In addition, because of the volume, not all decisions of intermediate state courts of appeals are published. Those that are, and all decisions of the state supreme court, appear in one of West Publishing Company's regional reporters and, if the state has one, the state's official reporter.

d.   Other Courts

There are also several other court systems. As sovereign entities, many Native American tribes have their own judicial systems, as does the United States military.

§ 2.2   The Relationship Between the Federal and State Governments

It is not enough, however, to look at our system of government only from the perspective of its three branches. To understand the system, you must also understand the relationship between the federal and state governments.

§ 2.2.1   A Short History

Like most things, our system of government is the product of our history. From the early 1600s until 1781, the "united states" were not united. Instead, the "country" was composed of independent colonies, all operating under different charters and each having its own laws and legal system. Although the colonies traded with each other, the relationship among the colonies was no closer than the relationship among the European countries prior to 1992. It was not until the Articles of Confederation were adopted in 1781 that the "states" ceded any of their rights to a federal government.

Even though the states ceded more rights when the Constitution became effective in 1789, they preserved most of their own law. Each state retained its own executive, its own legislature and laws, and its own court system.

Thus, our system of government is really two systems, a federal system and the fifty state systems, with the United States Constitution brokering the relationship between the two.

§ 2.2.2   The Relationship Between Laws Enacted by Congress and Those Enacted by the State Legislatures

As citizens of the United States, we are subject to two sets of laws: federal law and the law of the state in which we are citizens (or in which we act).

Most of the time, there is no conflict between these two sets of laws: federal law governs some conduct; state law, other conduct. For example, federal law governs bankruptcy proceedings, and state law governs divorce.

Occasionally, however, both Congress and a state legislature enact laws governing the same conduct. Sometimes these laws coexist. For example, both Congress and the states have enacted drug laws. Acting under the powers granted to it under the Commerce Clause, Congress has made it illegal to import controlled substances or to transport them across state lines. The states, acting consistently with the powers reserved to them, have made illegal the possession or sale of controlled substances within the state. In such instances, citizens are subject to both laws. A defendant may be charged under federal law with transporting a drug across state lines and under state law with possession.

There are times, however, when federal and state law do not complement each other and cannot coexist. An act can be legal under federal law but illegal under state law. In such instances, federal law preempts state law, provided that the federal law is constitutional. As provided in the Supremacy Clause, laws enacted by Congress under the powers granted to it under the Constitution are the "supreme Law of the Land; and the Judges in every State shall be bound thereby. . . ."

The issue is different when the conflicting laws are from different states. Although there are more and more uniform laws (the Uniform Child Custody Act, the Uniform Commercial Code), an activity that is legal in one state may be illegal in another state. For instance, although prostitution is legal in Nevada as a local option, it is illegal in other states.

§ 2.2.3   The Relationship Between Federal and State Courts

The relationship between the federal and state court systems is complex. Although each system is autonomous, in certain circumstances the state courts may hear cases brought under federal law, and the federal courts may hear cases brought under state law.

For example, although the majority of cases heard in state courts are brought under state law, state courts also have jurisdiction when a case is brought under a provision of the United States Constitution, a treaty, and certain federal statutes. Similarly, although the majority of cases heard in the federal courts involve questions of federal law, the federal courts have jurisdiction over cases involving questions of state law when the parties are from different states (diversity jurisdiction).

The appellate jurisdiction of the courts is somewhat simpler. In the federal system, the United States Court of Appeals has appellate jurisdiction to review the decisions of the United States District Courts and certain administrative agencies, and the United States Supreme Court is the court of last resort, having the power to review the decisions of the lower federal courts. Similarly, if a state has an intermediate court of appeals, that court has the power to review the decisions of the lower courts within its geographic jurisdiction, and the state's highest, or supreme court, is the court of last resort.

§ 2.2.4   The Relationship Among Federal, State, and Local Prosecutors

The power to prosecute cases arising under the United States Constitution and federal statutes is vested in the Department of Justice, which is headed by the Attorney General of the United States, a presidential appointee. Assisting the United States Attorney General are the United States Attorneys for each federal judicial district. The individual United States Attorneys' offices have two divisions: a civil division and a criminal division. The civil division handles civil cases arising under federal law, and the criminal division handles cases involving alleged violations of federal criminal statutes.

At the state level, the system is slightly different. In most states, the attorney for the state is the state attorney general, usually an elected official. Working for the state attorney general are a number of assistant attorneys general. However, unlike the United States attorneys, most state attorneys general do not handle criminal cases. Their clients are the various state agencies. For example, an assistant attorney general may be assigned to a state's department of social and health services, the department of licensing, the consumer protection bureau, or the department of workers' compensation, providing advice to the agency and representing the agency in civil litigation.

Criminal prosecutions are handled by county and city prosecutors. Each county has its own prosecutor's office, which has both a civil and a criminal division. Attorneys working for the civil division play much the same role as state assistant attorneys general. They represent the county and its agencies, providing both advice and representation. In contrast, the attorneys assigned to the criminal division are responsible for prosecutions under the state's criminal code. The county prosecutor's office decides whom to charge and then tries the cases.

Like the counties, cities have their own city attorney's office, which, at least in large cities, has civil and criminal divisions. Attorneys working in the civil division advise city departments and agencies and represent the city in civil litigation; attorneys in the criminal division prosecute criminal cases brought under city ordinances. State, county, and city prosecutors do not represent federal departments or agencies, nor do they handle cases brought under federal law.

§ 2.3   A Final Comment

Although there are numerous other ways of analyzing the United States system of government, these two perspectives — the three-branches perspective and the federal-state perspective — are the foundation on which the rest of your study of law will be built. Without such a foundation, without a thorough understanding of the interrelationships among the parts of the system, many of the concepts that you will encounter in law school would be difficult to learn. This is particularly true of legal writing. If you do not have a good understanding of the United States system of government, you will find it difficult to do legal research and legal analysis. Consequently, if you have questions about the United States system of government, this is the time to ask those questions. A question asked now will make the next three years much easier.

Chapter 2 Quiz

Draft answers for each of the following questions. Make your points clearly and concisely, and write sentences that are easy to read and that are grammatical and correctly punctuated.

1. Which branch of the federal government has the power to enact statutes?
2. Which branch of the federal government is responsible for enforcing federal statutes?
3. Which branch of the federal government has the power to determine whether a federal statute is constitutional?
4. What is the difference between a statute and a regulation?
5. At trial, what is the role of the judge? The role of the jury?
6. What role do the appellate courts play?
   a. Do they hear testimony?
   b. Do they decide issues of fact?
   c. Do they determine whether there was sufficient evidence to support the trial court's judgment?
   d. Do they determine whether the trial court applied the right law and applied that law correctly?
7. In the federal system, what is the name of the trial court? The intermediate court of appeals? What courts operate in your state? (To find this information, you will need to do an Internet search.)
8. What do lawyers and judges mean when they say that a federal statute "preempts" a state statute?
9. What do lawyers and judges mean when they say that a court has "jurisdiction" to hear a particular type of case?
10. Are all of the court decisions that appear on the Internet (for example, on Lexis Advance and WestlawNext) "published" decisions? What makes a decision a "published opinion"?

Introduction to Legal Research

M ost law students love doing legal research: They love being given a question and the opportunity and resources to explore that question. However, before you can do thorough and efficient research, you need to know what sources are available, how to find information in those sources, and how much weight to give to the information that you find. In addition, you need to know which of those sources are "free" and which are not.

§ 3.1   The Sources

Most law librarians refer to four types of sources: (1) sources that contain primary authority, (2) sources that contain secondary authority, (3) finding tools, and (4) citators. Although some sources have just one type of information, other sources have several types. For example, you may be able to use a single source as a finding tool and as a source for primary and secondary authority.

§ 3.1.1   Sources Containing Primary Authority

Primary authority is the law itself. For example, federal and state constitutions, federal and state statutes, federal and state regulations, federal and state cases, and federal and state court rules are all primary authority. In addition, at the local level, county and city charters and county and city ordinances are primary authority. Table 3.1 lists the types of primary authorities. (The

Table 3.1	**List of Primary Authorities**		
	Federal Law	**State Law**	**Local Law**
Constitutions	United States Constitution	State constitutions	County or city charter
Statutes	• *Statutes at Large* • *United States Code* • *United States Code Annotated* • *United States Code Service*	State session laws State codes (official and unofficial)	County or city ordinances
Regulations	*Code of Federal Regulations*	State regulations	Department or agency rules and procedures
Cases	United States Supreme Court decisions • *United States Reports* • *Supreme Court Reporter* • *United States Supreme Court Reports, Lawyers' Edition*	Decisions from the state's highest appellate court	Decisions by local departments, agencies, and courts
	United States Courts of Appeals decisions • *Federal Reporter* • *Federal Reporter, Second Series* • *Federal Reporter, Third Series*	Decisions from the state's intermediate level appellate court or courts	
	United States District Courts decisions • *Federal Supplement* • *Federal Supplement, Second Series* • *Federal Rules Decisions* • Specialized reporters	Decisions from state trial courts (as a general rule, these decisions are not published)	
Court Rules	Federal rules	State rules	Local rules

sources in which you can find these authorities are described in more detail in Chapters 4 through 9.)

Most primary authorities are available both in book and electronic formats. For instance, you can find federal statutes in four different sets of books (*Statutes at Large*, *United States Code*, *United States Code Annotated*, and *United States Code Service*) and on a number of different free and fee-based websites.

§ 3.1.2 Sources Containing Secondary Authority

Secondary authorities summarize, analyze, or comment on the law. As a researcher, you will use secondary authorities in two different ways: At the beginning of a research project, you will use secondary authorities to familiar-

Table 3.2	**List of Secondary Authorities**		
	Federal Issues	**State Issues**	**Local Issues**
Secondary sources that can be used for background reading	• Government websites • Federal practice books • Hornbooks • *Nutshells* • Legal encyclopedias	• Government websites • State practice books • Hornbooks • *Nutshells* • Legal encyclopedias	• Local websites • State practice books • Hornbooks • *Nutshells* • Legal encyclopedias
Secondary sources that can be used to gain a more sophisticated understanding of a particular issue	• Law reviews • Treatises • Looseleaf services • *American Law Reports* (A.L.R.) • A.L.R. Fed. • A.L.R. Fed. 2d	• Law reviews • Treatises • *American Law Reports* (A.L.R.) • A.L.R.4th • A.L.R.5th • A.L.R.6th	• Law reviews • Treatises • *American Law Reports* (A.L.R.) • A.L.R.4th • A.L.R.5th • A.L.R.6th

ize yourself with the issue that you have been asked to research, and near the end of the project you will sometimes use them to gain a more sophisticated understanding of the issue. For example, if you are asked to research a federal statute, you might begin your research by reading about the statute on a free government website that summarizes and explains that particular statute. Then, after you have located and analyzed the applicable primary authorities, you might look for a law review article or treatise that discusses that statute.

Table 3.2 lists some of the secondary authorities that are available. (See Chapters 5 through 9 for a more detailed discussion of these authorities and the Glossary for brief descriptions.)

Like primary authorities, most secondary authorities are available both in books and on free or fee-based websites.

§ 3.1.3   Finding Tools

Finding tools are what the name suggests: tools that help you locate primary and secondary authorities. Some examples of finding tools are annotated codes, digests, and search engines. Table 3.3 shows some of the finding tools that you can use to find primary and secondary authorities. (For a more detailed discussion of these authorities, see Chapters 4 through 9; for brief descriptions, see the Glossary.)

§ 3.1.4   Citators

Citators are used in two ways: (1) to determine whether a particular source, for example, a case, is still good law; and (2) to locate additional authorities that might be on point.

Historically, there was only one citator, and that was the book version of *Shepard's*®. Today, however, most libraries have canceled their subscriptions to the book version of *Shepard's*. Instead, most attorneys use the electronic version

Table 3.3	**List of Finding Tools**
	Finding Tools
Statutes	• Subject indexes in codes • References to statutes in cases, practice manuals, hornbooks, law review articles, and other secondary sources • Subject indexes and table of contents searches on fee-based services such as Lexis Advance®, WestlawNext™, and Bloomberg Law • Searches on fee-based services such as Lexis Advance, WestlawNext, and Bloomberg Law • Bing, Google, and other free search engines
Cases	• References to cases in other cases, practice manuals, hornbooks, law review articles, and other secondary sources • Digests • *American Law Reports* (A.L.R.) • Searches on Lexis Advance, WestlawNext, and Bloomberg Law • Citators, for example, Shepard's® and KeyCite® • Bing, Google, and other free search engines
Secondary Authorities	• Cross-references in annotated codes • References in cases, practice manuals, law review articles, and other secondary sources • Directories and database lists on fee-based services such as Lexis Advance, WestlawNext, and Bloomberg Law • Citators, for example, Shepard's, KeyCite, and BCite • Bing, Google, and other free search engines

of *Shepard's*, which is on Lexis Advance; KeyCite, which is on WestlawNext, or BCite, which is on Bloomberg Law. (For a more complete description of citators, see Chapter 10.)

Exercise 3A	**Primary Sources, Secondary Sources, and Finding Tools**

Go into your law library and locate each of the following sources. Select a volume and page through it, identifying the types of information contained in the source. Then write down the shelf location and two or three sentences describing the types of information contained in that source and how it is organized (chronological, alphabetical, topical). Be sure to include the entity that publishes the source. Note how the source is updated and whether it is an official or unofficial source. Also note what the source does not contain.

    I.   Primary Sources
        A. *United States Code*
        B. *Code of Federal Regulations*
        C. *United States Reports*
        D. *Federal Reporter, Third Series*
        E. *Federal Supplement, Second Series*

II. Secondary Sources
  A. A hornbook of your choice
  B. C.J.S. or Am. Jur. 2d
  C. A.L.R. Fed.
  D. A volume of your law school's law review
III. Finding Tools
  A. *United States Code Annotated*
  B. *Federal Practice Digest 4th*

§ 3.2 Using Citations to Locate Information in Books and Fee-Based Services

In addition to knowing what sources are available, you also need to know how to locate those sources. The key to this step is learning how to read and use legal citations.

Although there are a number of different citation systems,[1] each of these systems requires similar types of information in a similar order.

> **PRACTICE POINTER** In recent years, some jurisdictions have adopted a public domain. For a list of jurisdictions that have adopted such a format, see *http://www.abanet .org/tech/ltrc/research/citation/uscourts.html#wi.*

§ 3.2.1 Citations to Constitutional Provisions, Statutes, Regulations, and Court Rules

a. Constitutional Provisions

Most citations to constitutional provisions contain two types of information: an abbreviation that identifies the constitution and a number or set of numbers that identify a particular article, section, or amendment. In Example 1, the abbreviation tells you that the citation is to the United States Constitution, and the number tells you that it is a reference to a particular article and section within that article.[2]

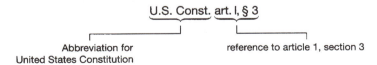

U.S. Const. art. I, § 3

Abbreviation for
United States Constitution

reference to article 1, section 3

---

1. The two most commonly used citation systems are set out in the *ALWD Citation Manual* and *The Bluebook*. Some states also have their own citation systems. To determine which system is used in your state, go to your state's court rules, which are available online.

2. The citations in this chapter comply with the rules for memoranda and briefs set out in both the *ALWD Citation Manual* and *The Bluebook*.

b.   Statutes and Regulations

Like the citations to constitutional provisions, most citations to statutes and regulations contain two types of information: an abbreviation that identifies the "code" in which the statute or regulation can be found and a number or numbers that identify the specific section. Depending on the jurisdiction, these numbers may include a reference to the title, chapter, and section or to just the title and section.

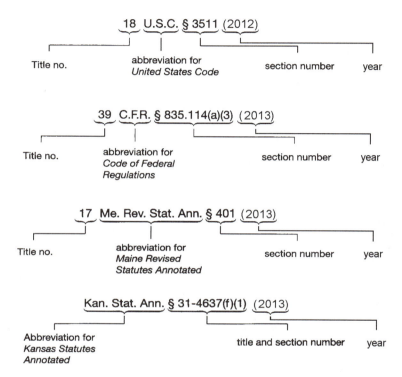

PRACTICE POINTER   In this context, the word "title" refers to a subject area. For example, in the *United States Code*, Title 11 sets out federal statutes relating to bankruptcy, Title 17 sets out the federal statutes relating to copyrights, and Title 29 sets out federal statutes relating to labor. In some states, the citation may include a reference to the title, to the chapter within that title, and to the specific subsection.

c.   Court Rules

Most citations to court rules include an abbreviation that identifies the set of rules and a number that identifies the specific rule.

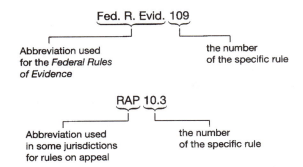

§ 3.2.2   Citations to Cases

Citations to cases contain more information. In addition to giving you the name of the case, most case citations include an abbreviation that identifies the reporter, or set of books, in which the case has been published; the volume number; and the page number. This information is usually set out in the following order:

case name,   vol. no.,   reporter,   page no.   (court and year of decision)

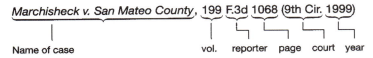

If the case appears in more than one reporter, the citation may also contain a parallel citation, that is, a reference to the other reporters in which the same case appears. For example, the United States Supreme Court's decision in *Terry v. Ohio* appears in three reporters, *United States Reports, Supreme Court Reporter,* and *United States Supreme Court Reports, Lawyers' Edition Second.* The first reference is to the official reporter, and the second and third references are parallel cites to unofficial reporters.

In addition to setting out the page on which the opinion begins, there may be a pinpoint cite (also known as a jump cite) that refers the reader to a specific page in the opinion. For instance, the next citation tells readers that the Ninth Circuit's decision in *Humanitarian Law Project* can be found in volume 352 of the *Federal Reporter, Third Series,* that the first page of the case is on page 382, and that the language that the author has quoted or relied on is on page 390.

Humanitarian Law Project v. United States Dep't of Justice, 352 F.3d 382, 390 (9th Cir. 2003)

Finally, if there was a subsequent opinion in the same case, the citation may include that subsequent history. In the following example, the *"aff'd"* and the reference to volume 509 of the *Federal Reporter, Third Series,* is the subsequent history.

Humanitarian Law Project v. Gonzales, 380 F. Supp. 2d 1134 (C.D. Cal. 2005), *aff'd, Humanitarian Law Project v. Mukasey*, 509 F.3d 1122 (9th Cir. 2007)

PRACTICE POINTER	In the preceding example, the case name changed when a new Attorney General was appointed.

Exercise 3B   **Reading Citations**

Translate each of the following citations. What does each of the numbers and letters mean?

1. 18 U.S.C. § 2339B (2012).
2. *Humanitarian Law Project v. United States Dep't of Justice*, 382 F.3d 1154 (9th Cir. 2004).
3. Randolph N. Jonakait, *The Mens Rea for the Crime of Providing Material Resources to a Foreign Terrorist Organization*, 56 Baylor L. Rev. 861 (2004).

§ 3.2.3   Using the Citations to Find Material in a Book

To find a statute, regulation, case, or secondary authority in your law library, use your library's user's guide, website, or electronic card catalog to find where the particular set of books or book is shelved in your library. Once you find the set, use the citation to find the particular statute, case, or section. For example, if you are looking for a statute, find the volume that contains the title set out in your citation, and then look through that volume to find the applicable section or the appropriate chapter and section. Similarly, if you are looking for a case, locate the correct reporter, and then use the citation's volume number to find the right volume. Once you have found the right volume, use the page number to find the case.

PRACTICE POINTER	Although once in practice you may not do your research in books, taking some time now to look at the books will help you understand the citations that you will see as you do your research and the types of information that are in different sources.

Exercise 3C   **Using Citations to Find Materials in Books**

Go into the law library and find each of the following sources.

1. What is the title of the statute that is at 18 U.S.C. § 2339B (2012)?
2. What is the name of the case that is at 314 F. Supp. 2d 279 (S.D.N.Y. 2004)?
3. What is the name of the law review article that is at 41 San Diego L. Rev. 839 (2004)?

§ 3.2.4   Using Citations to Find Material on a Free Website or Fee-Based Service Such as Lexis Advance, WestlawNext, or Bloomberg Law

If you have the citation, you can use that citation to find a copy of the statute, regulation, case, or secondary authority on Lexis Advance®, WestlawNext™, or Bloomberg Law. For step-by-step instructions, see *http://www.aspenlawschool.com/books/oates_legalwritinghandbook/*.

Exercise 3D	**Using Citations to Find Materials in Fee-Based Services**

Using Lexis Advance or WestlawNext, find and capture a screenshot showing the first page of each of the following documents.

1. The statute that is at 8 U.S.C. § 1158 (2012).
2. The case that is at 400 F.3d 785 (9th Cir. 2004).
3. The law review article that is at 82 St. John's L. Rev. 609 (2008).

---

§ 3.3   Deciding How Much Weight to Give to a Particular Authority

Not all enacted and common law is given equal weight. In deciding which law to apply, courts distinguish between mandatory and persuasive authority.

Mandatory authority is law that is binding on the court deciding the case. The court must apply that law. In contrast, persuasive authority is law that is not binding. Although the court may look to that law for guidance, it need not apply it.

Determining whether a particular statute or case is mandatory or persuasive authority is a two-step process. You must first determine which jurisdiction's law applies (that is, whether federal or state law applies and, if state law applies, which state's law); you must then determine which of that jurisdiction's statutes and cases are binding on the court that will be deciding the case.

§ 3.3.1   Which Jurisdiction's Law Applies?

Sometimes determining which jurisdiction's law applies is easy. For example, common knowledge (and common sense) tells you that federal law probably governs whether a federal PLUS loan constitutes income for federal income tax purposes. Similarly, you would probably guess that a will executed in California by a California resident would be governed by California state law. At other times, though, the determination is much more difficult. You probably would not know which jurisdiction's law governs a real estate contract between a resident of New York and a resident of Pennsylvania for a piece of property located in Florida.

Although the rules governing the determination of which jurisdiction's law applies are beyond the scope of this book (they are studied in Civil Procedure, Federal Courts, and Conflicts), keep two things in mind.

First, remember that in our legal system, federal law almost always preempts, or takes precedence over, state law. Consequently, if there is both a federal and a state statute on the same topic, the federal statute will preempt the state statute to the extent that the two are inconsistent. For example, if a federal statute makes it illegal to discriminate on the basis of familial status when renting an apartment but under a state statute such discrimination is lawful, the federal statute governs — it is illegal to discriminate on the basis of familial status. There are a few instances, however, when a state constitutional provision or a state statute will govern. If the state constitution gives a criminal defendant more rights than does the federal constitution, the state constitution applies. While states can grant an individual more protection, they cannot take away or restrict rights granted by the federal constitution or a federal statute.

Second, in the federal system there is not the same body of common law that there is in the states. Unlike the state systems, in the federal system there are no common law rules governing adverse possession or intentional torts such as assault and battery, false imprisonment, or the intentional infliction of emotional distress. As a consequence, if the cause of action is based on a common law doctrine, the case is probably governed by state and not federal law.

§ 3.3.2   What "Law" Will Be Binding on the Court?

Within each jurisdiction, the authorities are ranked. The United States Constitution is the highest authority, binding both state and federal courts. Other federal and state law is under the United States Constitution.

In the federal system, the highest authority is the Constitution. Under the Constitution are the federal statutes and regulations, and under the federal statutes and regulations are the cases interpreting and applying them.

In the state system, the ranking is similar. The highest authority is the state constitution, followed by state statutes and regulations and the cases interpreting and applying those statutes and regulations and state common law.

In addition, the cases themselves are ranked. In both the federal and state systems, decisions of the United States Supreme Court carry the most weight: When deciding a case involving the same law and similar facts, both the courts of appeals and the trial courts are bound by the decisions of the supreme, or highest, state courts. Decisions of intermediate courts of appeals come next; the trial courts under the jurisdiction of the intermediate courts of appeals are bound by the courts of appeals' decisions. At the bottom are the trial courts. Trial court decisions are binding only on the parties involved in the particular case.

Statutes and cases are also ranked by date. More recent statutes supersede earlier versions, and more recent common law rules supersede early rules by the same level court. Courts are bound by the highest court's most recent decision. For example, if there is a 1967 state intermediate court of appeals decision that makes an activity legal and a 1986 state supreme court decision that makes it illegal, in the absence of a statute, the 1986 supreme court decision governs. The 1986 decision would be mandatory authority, and all the courts within that jurisdiction would be bound by that decision.

Exercise 3E	**Mandatory and Persuasive Authority**

1. In 1930, in Case A, the Supreme Court of your state set out a common law rule. In 1956, in Case B, the Supreme Court of your state changed that rule. In your state, which case would be binding on a trial court: Case A or Case B?

2. Same facts as in Question 1 except that in 1981, in Case C, the Supreme Court of your state modified the rule set out in Case B, adding a requirement. In your state, which test would a trial court use: the test set out in Case A, the test set out in Case B, or the test set out in Case C?

Case A	State Supreme Court	1930
Case B	State Supreme Court	1956
Case C	State Supreme Court	1981

3. Same facts as in Question 2 except that in 1983 your state legislature enacted a statute that completely changed the common law rule. What is now binding on the trial court: the cases or the statute?

Case A	State Supreme Court	1930
Case B	State Supreme Court	1956
Case C	State Supreme Court	1981
State Statute		1983

4. Same facts as in Question 3 except that in 1985, in Case D, a case involving the application of the 1983 statute, the Court of Appeals of your state gives one of the words in the statute a broad interpretation. (The word was not defined in the statute.) In applying the statute, which courts are bound by the Court of Appeals' decision in Case D: a trial court within the Court of Appeals' geographic jurisdiction? A trial court outside the Court of Appeals' geographic jurisdiction? The division of the Court of Appeals that decided Case D? A division of the Court of Appeals other than the division that decided Case D? Your state's Supreme Court?

State Statute	1983
Case D	1985

5. In 1995, in Case E, a different division of the Court of Appeals applies the 1983 statute. In reaching its decision, the court declines to follow the decision in Case D. Instead of interpreting the word broadly, the court interprets it narrowly. The losing party disagrees with this decision and files an appeal with your state's Supreme Court. In deciding the appeal, is the Supreme Court bound by the Court of Appeals' decision in Case D? The Court of Appeals' decision in Case E?

State Statute		1983
Case D	Court of Appeals	1985
Case E	Court of Appeals	1995

6. Same facts as in Question 5 except that in 1999 the state legislature amends that statute, explicitly defining the word that was the subject of debate in Cases D and E. The legislature elects to give the word a very narrow meaning. In Case F, which is brought before a state trial court in 2008, what would be controlling: the 1983 version of the statute? The 1985 decision in Case D? The 1995 decision in Case E? The amended version of the statute?

   Note: In Case E, the Supreme Court reversed the Court of Appeals and interpreted the term broadly.

State Statute		1983
Case D	Court of Appeals	1985
Case E	Court of Appeals	1995
Case E	Supreme Court	1996
Amended State Statute		1999

Chapter 3 Quiz

Answer each of the following questions. For questions 2, 3, and 4, set out your answers using complete sentences. In doing so, make your points clearly and concisely, and write sentences that are easy to read and that are grammatical and correctly punctuated.

1. Which of the following sources are primary sources?
   a. United States Constitution
   b. State statutes
   c. United States Supreme Court decisions
   d. Law review articles
   e. Hornbooks
2. Are all primary sources mandatory authority? Why or why not?
3. What is a citator, and how is it used?
4. Where can you find a copy of the following case: *Herring v. United States*, 555 U.S. 135 (2009)?
5. In a case being decided by the Oregon Supreme Court, which of the following cases would be mandatory authority?
   a. An Oregon Supreme Court decision?
   b. A California Supreme Court decision?
   c. A decision from the Sixth Circuit Court of Appeals?

Researching Issues Governed by State Statutes, Federal Statutes, and Local Ordinances

Researching Issues Governed by State Statutes and Regulations

L earning to research issues governed by state statutes and regulations is a lot like learning to play chess. Although you can learn the names of the pieces and the standard moves relatively quickly, it takes a long time to become an expert. This chapter should, however, help you develop that expertise a bit more rapidly.

Before you begin reading this chapter, note that it has several components: (1) the text, which sets out basic information; (2) exercises, which ask you to apply what you have just read; (3) a quiz that tests the materials set out in the chapter; and (4) an electronic supplement, which shows you how to research an issue governed by a state statute using free sources, Lexis Advance®, WestlawNext™, Bloomberg Law, Lexis.com®, and Westlaw® Classic. To access the supplement, go to *http://www.aspenlawschool.com/books/oates_legalwriting handbook/*. Your access code to the website is on the card that came with the book. In the ebook, instructions for getting an access code are on the page immediately following the cover page.

§ 4.1 Research Plan for an Issue Governed by State Statutes

The research plan for issues governed by state statutes and regulations has four steps: (1) do background reading to familiarize yourself with the area of law; (2) locate and read primary sources; (3) cite check your primary sources to make sure that they are still good law; and (4) if appropriate, look for cases from other jurisdictions, law review articles, or other commentaries.

Research Plan for an Issue Governed by State Statutes

Jurisdiction: [Enter the name of the applicable state.]

Type of Law: Enacted law

Preliminary Issue

Statement: [Put your first draft of the issue statement here.]

Step 1:   If you are unfamiliar with the area of law, spend thirty to sixty minutes doing background reading.

Step 2:   Locate the governing statutes and regulations and the cases that have interpreted and applied those statutes and regulations.

Step 3:   Cite check the cases that you plan to use to make sure that they are still good law.

Step 4:   If appropriate, locate cases from other jurisdictions, law review articles, or other commentaries that might be on point.

§ 4.2   Sources for State Statutory Research

The first step is to learn what sources are available. Table 4.1 lists some, but not all, of the sources that you can use in researching an issue governed by state statutes and regulations. Note that because the names of the sources vary by state, we have listed the sources using generic labels rather than specific names. (For a list of the names of the sources in a particular state, see the listing for that state in Appendix 1 of the *ALWD Citation Manual* or Table 1 in *The Bluebook*.) Also note that not all states will have all the sources listed. For example, not all states have both an unannotated and an annotated code. Finally, note that many of the sources are available in book form, on free websites, and on fee-based services. In practice, you will need to decide which option is the best option.

§ 4.2.1   Sources for Background Reading

If you are familiar with the area of law that you have been asked to research, you can skip this step. If, however, the area is one that is new to you, begin your research by spending a few minutes doing background reading.

PRACTICE POINTER   In some situations, you will not need to do background reading. For example, if all you need is the text of the statute or a list of cases that have discussed the statute, you will not need to do background reading. Don't make the research harder than it needs to be. If, however, you are not sure which statute applies or even whether there is a governing statute, doing background reading will usually save you time and help you do more sophisticated analysis.

Table 4.1	**Sources of State Law**
	State Law
Background Reading	• State practice manuals • Hornbooks • *Nutshells* • The Internet
State Session Laws (statutes in order enacted)	• State session laws
State Codes (statutes organized by topic)	• Unannotated code • Annotated code
State Regulations	• Administrative code
Cases Interpreting and Applying Statutes	• State reporter setting out decisions from the state's highest appellate court • State reporter setting out decisions from the state's intermediate appellate courts • West regional reporter that contains decisions from the state's highest appellate court and the state's intermediate appellate courts and decisions from other courts in the same region.
Cite Checking	• KeyCite® • *Shepard's*® • BCite
Secondary Authorities	• Attorney general opinions • *American Law Reports* (for example, A.L.R.4th, A.L.R.5th, and A.L.R.6th) • Law review articles

a.   Practice Manuals and Practice Books

For issues governed by state law, the best source for background reading is almost always a state practice manual. In most states, these manuals are written by practitioners and provide the reader with an overview of the area of law and citations to key statutes, regulations, and cases. In addition, some practice manuals set out sample forms and practice pointers. Although most practice manuals are updated regularly, some are not. Therefore, always check to see when the manual that you are using was last updated.

Historically, most practice manuals were available only in book form. Today, however, many of these manuals are available on fee-based services. For example, practice manuals published by West, a Thomson Reuters business, are available on Westlaw Classic and WestlawNext, and some of the practice manuals are available on Lexis.com and Lexis Advance.

To find the book version of a practice manual, use your library's electronic card catalog and do key word searches using the name of the state and one or more of the following words: "practice," "procedure," and "manual." To find out what practice manuals are available on a particular fee-based service, check that service's list of databases or ask a colleague or your service's sales representative.

Exercise 4A	State Practice Manuals

Using your library's electronic card catalog, locate the names and call numbers for practice manuals for one of the following states:

1. California
2. Maine
3. Texas
4. The state in which your law school is located

b.   Hornbooks and *Nutshells*

If the practice manuals do not discuss the issue that you have been asked to research, look for a hornbook or a *Nutshell.* Hornbooks are one-volume hardbound books that provide the reader with an overview of an area of law, for example, civil procedure, contract law, property law, or tort law. *Nutshells* are shorter one-volume paperbacks designed primarily as a study tool for law students. Like hornbooks, *Nutshells* deal with broad areas of law. Although hornbooks and *Nutshells* will not tell you what the law is in your state, they can provide you with general information about the area of law. To find copies of hornbooks and *Nutshells,* use your library's electronic card catalog. For example, to find a *Nutshell,* do a title or key word search using the word "Nutshell" and a word or phrase describing the area of law.

Exercise 4B	Hornbooks and *Nutshells*

Using your library's electronic card catalog, locate the names and call numbers for hornbooks and *Nutshells* that discuss one of the following areas of law:

1. Civil Procedure
2. Property
3. Contracts
4. The area of law that you would like to practice

c.   The Internet

Increasingly, the Internet is a good source for doing background reading related to state statutes. To locate a website that discusses a particular statute, either use the citation to the statute as a search term or enter terms that relate to the area of law. If your search retrieves a number of websites, look first at government-sponsored sites (.gov), educational sites (.edu), and sites sponsored by reliable organizations (.org).

Exercise 4C   **Bing and Google**

Using either Bing or Google, locate and record the URL for one or more websites that provide background information about landlord-tenant law in one of the following states:

1. California
2. New York
3. Texas
4. The state in which your law school is located

---

§ 4.2.2   Sources for Statutes

Most state statutes come in three forms: in the state's session laws, in unannotated codes, and in annotated codes.

> **PRACTICE POINTER**   Although the session laws of some states can only be found in book form, you can find the *Statutes at Large* (the session laws for federal statutes) and unannotated and annotated versions of state and federal codes in both book and electronic formats.

a.   Session Laws

Session laws are the statutes published in the order in which they were enacted. At the end of a legislative session, the statutes enacted during that session are collected and arranged, not by topic, but by date. For instance, statutes enacted during the 2009 legislative session will be set out in date order in one volume, the statutes enacted during the 2010 legislative session will be set out in date order in another volume, and so on. To find a session law, you need to know when the statute was enacted and its number. In most state codes, that number is found at the end of the statute: The information set out in the "CREDIT(S)" section tells you when the statute was enacted and amended, and the chapter and section numbers tell you where you can find the original version of the statute and any amendments.

The only time that you will use session laws is when you are doing a legislative history. (See Chapter 11 in this book.) For other types of statutory research, use an unannotated or annotated code.

b.   Unannotated Codes

Statutes are "codified" when they are arranged, not in the order in which they were enacted, but by topic. Thus, in a code, all the statutes relating to a particular topic will be placed together. For instance, all the statutes relating to criminal law will be placed under one "title" or subject heading, all the statutes relating to marriage will be placed under another title or subject heading, and all the statutes relating to commercial transactions will be placed under yet another title or subject heading. The decision about where to place a particular statute is made not by the legislative body itself but by attorneys who work for the state as "code revisers."

Most unannotated codes set out only the text of the statutes, the credits, and historical notes. Therefore, think about using an unannotated code when all you want is the text of the statute. In particular, use an unannotated code when your issue is governed by several different statutory sections: Because there will not be any cross-references or Notes of Decisions between the sections, it will be easier to see how the various sections work together.

An unannotated code may be a state's official code or its unofficial code. Most unannotated codes are available both in book form and on both fee-based and free websites. For instance, if the unannotated code is the state's official code, you should be able to find a copy on the state's website.

> **PRACTICE POINTER**   As a practicing attorney, you will probably use your state's official website frequently. It is, therefore, a good idea to spend some time exploring that site to see what is and is not there. In addition, think about adding your state's website to your list of favorites.

c.   Annotated Codes

As you may have guessed, an annotated code is a code that has been annotated. In addition to setting out the text of the statutes, the credits, and historical notes, an annotated code also sets out cross-references to other sources published by the same publisher and Notes of Decisions (Westlaw Classic and WestlawNext) or Case Notes (Lexis.com and Lexis Advance), which are one-paragraph descriptions of cases that have cited the statute. Consequently, an annotated code is both primary authority[1] because it sets out the law itself and a finding tool because you can use it to find other primary authority, in this instance cases that have interpreted and applied the statute.

In the past, most states published their own unannotated codes, and private publishing companies published the annotated codes. Some states have stopped publishing the unannotated version of their state codes, however, and have entered into contracts with private publishing companies to make the publishing company's annotated code their official state code. For example, both Maine and New Jersey use the West versions of the code as their official codes. Annotated codes are available both in books and on Lexis.com, Lexis Advance, Westlaw Classic, and WestlawNext.

You should use an annotated code when you are interested not only in the text of the statute but also in how the courts have interpreted and applied the statute. Read the statute; determine which elements, or requirements, are likely to be in dispute; and then locate cases that have discussed those elements, or requirements, using the Notes of Decisions or Case Notes.

---

1. For a definition of the terms "primary authority," "secondary authority," and "finding tools," see Chapter 3 or the Glossary at the end of the book.

PRACTICE POINTER	Most citation systems require you to cite to the official rather than unofficial version of the code unless the material that you are citing appears in only the unofficial version. See Rule 14.1 in the

ALWD Citation Manual and Rule 12.2.1(a) in The Bluebook.

Exercise 4D	**State Statutes: The Names of State Codes**

Using the *ALWD Citation Manual* or *The Bluebook,* record the names of the unannotated codes and annotated codes that are published for the following states:

1. California
2. New York
3. Texas
4. The state in which your law school is located

§ 4.2.3   Sources for State Regulations

In enacting a state statute, the state legislature may grant a state administrative agency the power to promulgate regulations. When the proper procedures have been followed, those regulations have the effect of law and are, therefore, primary authority.

Although the process varies from state to state, in most states proposed regulations are first published in a state register and then in the state's administrative code. In most states, the register and the administrative code are available in both book form and on the state's website. In addition, the regulations are on fee-based and other free websites.

Exercise 4E	**State Regulations: The Names of State Administrative Codes**

Using the *ALWD Citation Manual* or *The Bluebook,* record the name of the administrative code for one of the following states:

1. California
2. New York
3. Texas
4. The state in which your law school is located

§ 4.2.4   Locating Cases That Have Interpreted or Applied a State Statute

a.   Notes of Decisions/Case Notes

When the statutory language, by itself, answers your question, you do not need to look for cases that have interpreted or applied the statute. However, when the statutory language is ambiguous, you will need to look for cases that have interpreted the statute. One of the easiest ways to find these cases is to use an annotated code.

As soon as they release an opinion, most courts send an electronic copy of their opinion to the publishing companies. When the Thomson West attorneys receive an opinion, they draft a one-sentence summary for each point of law set out in the opinion. When the summary appears at the beginning of an opinion, it is called a "headnote." When it appears after the text of a statute, it is called a "Note of Decision." LexisNexis uses a slightly different approach. Instead of drafting one-sentence summaries, the LexisNexis attorneys identify the key language and quote that key language at the beginning of the opinion in headnotes or, if the language relates to a statute, in Case Notes following the text of the statute.

If there are relatively few cases that have discussed a particular statute, these Notes of Decisions and Case Notes will be listed together after the statute. If, though, there are a number of cases that have discussed a particular statute, the Notes of Decisions and Case Notes will be organized by subtopics. Your job as a legal researcher is to read through the relevant Notes of Decisions and Case Notes and then locate and read the cases that appear to have the types of information that you need.

PRACTICE POINTER	As a general rule, decisions from higher courts will be listed before decisions from lower courts and, if there is more than one decision from a particular court, newer cases will be listed before older cases.

Although Notes of Decisions and Case Notes set out points of law, the notes are only finding tools and not something that you can rely on or cite to in a memo or a brief. Thus, use the Notes of Decisions and Case Notes as finding tools and not as authority.

Exercise 4F   **Locating State Statutes**

1. In the law library, locate the annotated code for one of the following states:

   a. Indiana
   b. Kentucky
   c. Massachusetts
   d. The state in which your law school is located

   Using the index, locate the statutory section or sections in your state's code that deal with security deposits for residential rentals. Once you have found the applicable statutory section or sections, list the types of information that follow the text of one of the sections. For example, are there historical notes? Cross-references to other sources? Notes of Decisions or Case Notes?

2. Read section 4.3.3 or 4.3.4 in the electronic supplement. For your state, how would you find the statutory section or sections dealing with security deposits for residential rentals? Once you

have found the applicable statutory section or sections, examine the information following the text of the statute. Is it the same information that you found in the book? Why or why not?

b.   Reporters

A "reporter" is a set of books in which court decisions are reported. In many states, the decisions of a state's highest court are placed in one reporter, and the decisions of a state's intermediate court of appeals are placed in a different reporter. For example, in Georgia, copies of the Supreme Court of Georgia's opinions are published in *Georgia Reports*, and copies of the Georgia Court of Appeals' decisions are published in *Georgia Appeals Reports*. In addition, both Georgia Supreme Court and Georgia Court of Appeals decisions are published in a regional reporter, the *South Eastern Reporter*, which is published by West and is part of West's National Reporter System. For a map showing which states' opinions are published in which regional reporter, see *http://lawschool.westlaw .com/federalcourt/NationalReporterPage.asp.*

When the decisions of a particular court are published in more than one reporter, one of those reporters will be designated as the official reporter, and the other reporter(s) will be designated as the unofficial reporter(s). For example, in Georgia, *Georgia Reports* and *Georgia Appeals Reports* are the official reporters and *South Eastern Reporter* is the unofficial reporter.

In other states, the decisions of both the state's highest court and intermediate court of appeals are published in the same state reporter. For instance, in New Mexico, the decisions of both the New Mexico Supreme Court and the New Mexico Court of Appeals are published in *New Mexico Reports*. In addition, the decisions of both the New Mexico Supreme Court and the New Mexico Court of Appeals are published in the *Pacific Reporter*, which is another one of West's regional reporters.

Still other states have stopped publishing their own reporters. In these states, the state's decisions can only be found in the regional reporter. For instance, since 1968, Iowa decisions have been published in only the *North Western Reporter*.

PRACTICE POINTER	To find the names of the reporters in which a particular court's decisions are published, see Appendix 1 in the *ALWD Citation Manual* or Table 1 of *The Bluebook*.

Exercise 4G	**The Names of State Reporters**

Using the *ALWD Citation Manual* or *The Bluebook,* identify the names of reporters in which the current decisions of the following courts are published.

1. Current decisions of the Idaho Supreme Court are published in _____
    _____.

2. Current decisions of the Massachusetts Supreme Judicial Court are published in _____
    _____.

3. Current decisions of New Mexico Court of Appeals are published in _____

_____.

Like session laws (see section 4.2.2.a), reporters are organized chronologically. Cases decided in 1995 appear before cases that were decided in 2000, and cases that were decided in 2009 appear before cases that were decided in 2013. In addition, a case that was decided on May 20 will appear before one that was decided on May 21.

> **PRACTICE POINTER**   When two cases are published in the same reporter, you can use the citation to determine which case is the most recent: The case with the highest volume number is the most recent case. Similarly, if the cases appear not only in the same reporter but also in the same volume of that reporter, the case with the highest page number will be the most recent case.

To find a case in the book version of a reporter, you need three pieces of information: (1) the name of the reporter, (2) the volume in which the case appears, and (3) the page on which the case begins. This information is buried in the citation that appears at the end of each Note of Decision/Case Note. Look, for example, at the following citation, which is taken from the Notes of Decisions following section 48.031 of the *Florida Statutes Annotated*, a West publication.

Busman v. State, Dept. of Revenue, App. 3 Dist., 905 So. 2d 956 (2005).

Although this citation is not in the form specified by either the *ALWD Citation Manual* or *The Bluebook*, it does give you the information that you need to find the case. This citation tells you that the court's opinion in *Busman v. State, Dept. of Revenue* can be found in volume 905 of the *Southern Reporter, Second Series*, beginning on page 956. In addition, the citation tells you that the opinion was issued in 2005 and that the case was heard and decided by the Third District Appellate Court. Because the citation appears in the annotation to the Florida statutes, you can infer that the case is a Florida case. For more on reading citations, see section 3.2 in Chapter 3.

> **PRACTICE POINTER**   It is not uncommon for a publishing company to use its own citation rules and not the citation rules in the *ALWD Citation Manual* or *The Bluebook*. If, however, you are citing the case in a memo or brief, you need to use the citation rules used in your jurisdiction and not the publishing company's rules. In other words, do not just copy and paste the citation into your memo or brief without first making sure that the citation complies with your jurisdiction's citation rules.

You can find a copy of a published decision in a number of places: (1) if the state publishes its own reporter, in that reporter; (2) in the applicable regional reporter; (3) on fee-based services, for example, Lexis.com, Lexis Advance, Westlaw Classic, WestlawNext, and Bloomberg Law; and (4) on free websites, for example, Google® Scholar.

Exercise 4H	**Locating Cases**

Select one of the following cases, and then locate a copy of the case in the official reporter (a book), in the regional reporter (a book), and on Lexis Advance, WestlawNext, and Google Scholar. Compare the text of the opinions. Are they the same or different? Compare the "editorial features." Are the headnotes the same or different? For instructions on how to locate cases using Google Scholar, Lexis Advance, and WestlawNext, see 4.3.2, 4.3.3, and 4.3.4 in the electronic supplement.

1. *State v. Lambert*, 175 Vt. 275, 830 A.2d 9 (2003).
2. *People v. Bell*, 264 Mich. App. 58, 689 N.W.2d 732 (2004).
3. A case selected by your professor.

---

§ 4.2.5   Sources for Secondary Materials

When the statute, regulations, and in-state cases do not answer the question that you were asked to research, you may need to look at cases from other jurisdictions or at secondary sources.

a.   State Attorney General Opinions

As we explained in Chapter 2, the state attorney general is the state's attorney. As the attorney for the governor, the legislature, and state agencies, the state attorney general will sometimes prepare written opinions that analyze, explain, or evaluate a state statute or regulation. While these opinions do not have the effect of law, they do provide insight into how the state believes the statute or regulation should be interpreted and applied.

In most states, the state attorney general opinions are available on the state's website.

b.   American Law Reports

American Law Reports (A.L.R.) was first published in 1919 to compete with West's National Reporter System. However, instead of publishing every state and federal opinion, A.L.R. was selective and published only those cases that it deemed to be "significant." For each of these significant cases, it included an annotation that collected and discussed other cases that dealt with the issue raised in the significant case.

Today, researchers use A.L.R. not as a source for the text of an opinion but for its annotations. In particular, researchers use A.L.R. as a finding tool to locate summaries of cases from around the country that deal with a particular issue of law.

Like other reporters, A.L.R. is arranged chronologically. Annotations dealing with state issues are set out in A.L.R., A.L.R.2d, A.L.R.3d, A.L.R.4th, A.L.R.5th, and A.L.R.6th. Annotations dealing with federal issues are set out in A.L.R. Fed. or A.L.R. Fed. 2d.

A.L.R.	1919-1948
A.L.R.2d	1948-1965
A.L.R.3d	1965-1980
A.L.R.4th	1980-1991
A.L.R.5th	1992-2005
A.L.R.6th	2005-current
A.L.R. Fed.	1969-2005
A.L.R. Fed. 2d	2005-current

A.L.R. is available both in book form and on Lexis.com, Lexis Advance, Westlaw Classic, and WestlawNext. The books have subject indexes.

> **PRACTICE POINTER**   Because you want the most current information, look first for annotations published in A.L.R.5th and A.L.R.6th. In addition, if you are using the book version, be sure to check the "pocket parts," that is, the inserts at the back of the book, for more recent cases.

c. Law Reviews and Journals

Law reviews and journals publish articles written by law school professors, judges, practitioners, and law students. While most law reviews and journals are published by law schools, some are published by organizations.

Occasionally, you will find a law review article that analyzes the state statute that governs your case or that analyzes one of the cases that has interpreted and applied that statute. In addition, occasionally you will find a law review article that analyzes an identically or similarly worded statute from another state. In these instances, the law review article can provide you with an analysis of the statute, the history of the statute, and possible arguments.

Some law review articles are now available for free. To look for articles, see the American Bar Association's website (*http://www.americanbar.org/groups/ departments_offices/legal_technology_resources/resources/free_journal_ search.html*), SSRN (*http://papers.ssrn.com/sol3/DisplayAbstractSearch.cfm*), or Google Scholar (*http://scholar.google.com/schhp?hl=en&as_sdt=0,48*).

In addition, you can find copies of law review articles using Lexis.com, Lexis Advance, Westlaw Classic, or WestlawNext. If your search retrieves more than one document, look first at the articles published in law reviews or journals from your state's law schools. Most of the articles that deal with a specific state statute are published in the law reviews and journals of that state's law schools.

§ 4.3   Using the Research Plan to Research an Issue Governed by State Statutes

In researching an issue governed by a state statute, you will usually use a combination of free sources and fee-based services. For example, if all you need is the text of a statute, you should locate the text of that statute using the state's legislature's website. If, however, you also need to find cases that have interpreted and applied that statute, you may want to use the Case Notes that are on Lexis Advance or the Notes of Decision that are on WestlawNext. You can, however, then download and read the cases for free using Google Scholar.

The bottom line is that to be an effective researcher you need to know how to use a variety of tools. Thus, before you go into practice you should familiarize yourself with the free websites and the fee-based services that are currently available, comparing and contrasting the advantages and disadvantages of each.

> **PRACTICE POINTER**   You should be able to do most statutory research using free sources: State and federal statutes are available on free government websites that are both reliable and up-to-date. In addition, you can find the text of cases that have cited a statute using free websites. You may, though, want to use an annotated code to find cases, which means that you will need to use Lexis Advance, WestlawNext, Lexis.com, or Westlaw Classic. (At this point, Bloomberg Law does not have an annotated code.) In addition, you will need to cite check any cases that you use from *Shepard*'s, KeyCite, or BCite, which is on Bloomberg Law.

To learn more about using free and fee-based services to research issues governed by state statutes, see the electronic supplement at http://www.aspen-lawschool.com/books/oates_legalwritinghandbook/.

§ 4.3.1   The Assignment
§ 4.3.2   Researching an Issue Governed by State Statutes and Regulations Using Free Websites
§ 4.3.3   Researching an Issue Governed by State Statutes and Regulations Using Lexis Advance
§ 4.3.4   Researching an Issue Governed by State Statutes and Regulations Using WestlawNext
§ 4.3.5   Researching an Issue Governed by State Statutes and Regulations Using Bloomberg Law
§ 4.3.6   Researching an Issue Governed by State Statutes and Regulations Using Lexis.com
§ 4.3.7   Researching an Issue Governed by State Statutes and Regulations Using Westlaw Classic

Chapter 4 Quiz

Draft answers for each of the following questions. Make your points clearly and concisely, and write sentences that are easy to read and that are grammatical and correctly punctuated.

1. What are practice manuals? Are practice manuals primary or secondary authority?
2. What are session laws? Are session laws law primary or secondary authority?
3. What does it mean to say the statutes have been "codified"?
4. What type of information does an unannotated code contain? An annotated code?
5. Under what circumstances can a state agency promulgate regulations?
6. What is one way to find cases that discuss a particular statute?
7. Can you cite to Notes of Decision? Who writes the Notes of Decision?
8. What is a reporter?
9. Are all court decisions published decisions?
10. What is an attorney general's opinion? Is an attorney general's opinion primary or secondary authority?

Researching Issues Governed by Federal Statutes and Regulations

The commentators are right. There is almost no area of the law or, for that matter, our lives, that is not regulated, at least in part, by federal statutes. Federal statutes regulate our food supply, the vehicles we drive, the schools we attend, and our working conditions. Thus, no matter what type of law you practice, you need to know how to research federal statutes and regulations.

In this chapter, you will learn how to modify the research plan presented in Chapter 1 so that it works for issues governed by federal statutes and regulations. In particular, you will learn about secondary sources that you can use to familiarize yourself with a particular federal act; how you can find the governing federal statutes and regulations and the cases that have applied those statutes and regulations; how you can determine whether the statutes, regulations, and cases you have found are still good law; and which secondary sources you can consult to gain a more sophisticated understanding of the issue you were asked to research.

Like the prior chapter, this chapter has several components: (1) the text, which sets out basic information; (2) exercises, which ask you to apply what you have just read; (3) a quiz that tests the materials set out in the chapter; and (4) an electronic supplement, which shows you how to research an issue governed by federal statutes and regulations using free sources, Lexis Advance®, WestlawNext™, Bloomberg Law, Lexis.com®, and Westlaw® Classic. To access the supplement, go to *http://www.aspenlawschool.com/books/oates_legalwrit inghandbook/*. Your access code to the website is on the card that came with the book. In the ebook, instructions for getting an access code are on the page immediately following the cover page.

§ 5.1   Research Plan for Issues Governed by Federal Statutes and Regulations

Like the research plan for issues governed by state statutes and regulations, the research plan for issues governed by federal statutes and regulations has four steps.

Research Plan for an Issue Governed by Federal Statutes and Regulations

Jurisdiction:	Federal
Type of Law:	Enacted law

Preliminary Issue
Statement: [Put your first draft of the issue statement here.]

Step 1:   If you are unfamiliar with the area of law, spend thirty to sixty minutes familiarizing yourself with the area of law by looking for information on the Internet, in a practice manual, in a hornbook, in a *Nutshell*, in a legal encyclopedia, or in another secondary source.

Step 2:   Locate, read, and analyze the applicable *United States Code* sections, the applicable *Code of Federal Regulations* sections, and cases that have interpreted or applied the applicable statutory sections and regulations.

Step 3:   Cite check the statutes, regulations, and cases to make sure they are still good law.

Step 4:   If appropriate, locate and read additional primary and secondary authorities.

§ 5.2   Sources for Federal Statutory Research

Before you begin researching a problem, you need to know what sources are available. Table 5.1 lists some of the sources that you can use in researching an issue governed by federal statutes and regulations. As you look at this list, note that some of these sources are available in book form; on fee-based services such as Lexis Advance, WestlawNext, and Bloomberg Law; and on free websites.

§ 5.2.1   Sources for Background Reading

a.   The Internet

For many issues governed by federal statutes, the best place to do your background reading is on the Internet. If you know the name of the act, select

Table 5.1	**Sources of Federal Law**
	FEDERAL LAW
Background Reading	• Internet • Practice manuals • Hornbooks • *Nutshells* • Legal encyclopedias
Session Laws (statutes in order enacted)	• *Statutes at Large* • *United States Code* (U.S.C.)
Codes (statutes organized by topics)	• *United States Code Annotated* (U.S.C.A.) • *United States Code Service* (U.S.C.S.)
Regulations	• *Code of Federal Regulations* (C.F.R.) • *Federal Register* (Fed. Reg.)
Cases Interpreting and Applying Statutes	• *Federal Supplement* (F. Supp. or F. Supp. 2d) (decisions from the United States District Courts) • *Federal Reporter* (F., F.2d, or F.3d) (decisions from the United States Courts of Appeals) • *United States Reports* (U.S.) (decisions from the United States Supreme Court) • *Supreme Court Reporter* (S. Ct.) (decisions from the United States Supreme Court) • *United States Supreme Court Reports, Lawyers' Edition* (L. Ed. or L. Ed. 2d) (decisions from the United States Supreme Court)
Cite Checking	• KeyCite • *Shepard's* • BCite
Secondary Authorities	• Law review articles • Treatises • Looseleaf services • *American Law Reports, Federal* (A.L.R. Fed. or A.L.R. Fed. 2d)

a search engine, and search for reliable websites that discuss that act. For example, if you are looking for information about the Americans with Disabilities Act, go to Bing, Google, or a similar search engine, and search for websites that contain the phrase "Americans with Disabilities Act." When the list appears, quickly review it, looking for websites that summarize the Americans with Disabilities Act. As a general rule, select government websites (.gov) over commercial websites (.com).

PRACTICE POINTER	If you do not know the name of the act, type in a word or words that describe your topic.

b.   Practice Manuals

Although most law firms, agencies, and courts have copies of their state's practice manuals in book form, they may not have federal practice manuals. Instead, they may purchase looseleaf services for the areas of law in which they practice and rely on fee-based services such as Lexis Advance, WestlawNext, or Bloomberg Law for their other needs. For example, a tax attorney might purchase the *CCH Standard Federal Tax Reporter*® and rely on fee-based services for everything else.

c.   Hornbooks and *Nutshells*

Hornbooks and *Nutshells* are one-volume books that provide the reader with an overview of an area of law. For example, the hornbook *Intellectual Property: The Law of Copyrights, Patents, and Trademarks* provides an overview of the various topics in intellectual property law. Similarly, the shorter, one-volume *Intellectual Property: Unfair Competition in a Nutshell* provides an overview of the law relating to unfair competition.

Note that most hornbooks and *Nutshells* deal with areas of law and not with specific federal acts. Therefore, as a general rule, use a hornbook or a *Nutshell* when you want to do background reading on an area of law, and use the Internet when you want to do background reading on a specific act.

> **PRACTICE POINTER**   You can use your library's electronic card catalog to find hornbooks and *Nutshells*. You can also ask the law librarian and practitioners for recommendations.

d.   Legal Encyclopedias

At one point, the book versions of legal encyclopedias were the source of choice for background reading. When asked to research an issue in an unfamiliar area of law, attorneys would go to one of the two legal encyclopedias, *American Jurisprudence* (Am. Jur.) or *Corpus Juris Secundum* (C.J.S.), and read the summary of the law.

Like the book versions of other more general encyclopedias, the book versions of Am. Jur. and C.J.S. are being used less and less often; the books are expensive to buy and update and take lots of space to store. Consequently, if the office in which you work has one of these encyclopedias, by all means use it. If, however, your office does not have Am. Jur. or C.J.S., another good source is WEX, a free online dictionary and legal encyclopedia sponsored and hosted by the Legal Information Institute at Cornell Law School. See *http://www.law.cornell.edu/wex/*.

> **Exercise 5A**   **Sources That Can Be Used to Find Background Reading**

1. Using Bing or Google, locate a government website that provides background information about the Clean Air Act of 1990. Make a screenshot of the page that provides readers with an overview of the Act.

2. Using Lexis Advance or WestlawNext, locate a practice manual that provides an overview of the Clean Air Act. Record the citation for the source and provide a one- or two-sentence description of the practice manual.
3. Using your library's electronic card catalog, locate an environmental law hornbook or Nutshell that provides background information about the Clean Air Act. Record the call number and write a one- or two-sentence description of the hornbook or *Nutshell*.
4. Look up "Clean Air Act" and "Environmental Law" in either the book or electronic version of Am. Jur. 2d or C.J.S. What do you find?

§ 5.2.2   Sources for Federal Statutes and Regulations

Federal statutes come in three forms. You can find the text of a particular federal act in the session laws, in the unannotated code, and in two annotated codes.

a.   Session Laws

Statutes at Large sets out federal statutes in the order in which they were enacted. At the end of each Congress, the statutes enacted during that Congress are collected and arranged, not by topic, but by date. For instance, statutes enacted during the 106th Congress will be printed in date order in one set of volumes, the statutes enacted during the 107th Congress will be printed in date order in another set of volumes, and the statutes enacted during the 108th Congress will be printed in yet another set of volumes. Therefore, to find a session law, you need to know the Congress during which the statute was enacted and the public law number.

PRACTICE POINTER	The only time that you will use session laws is when you are doing a legislative history. For other types of statutory research, use an unannotated or annotated code.

b.   Unannotated Codes

Statutes are "codified" when they are arranged, not in chronological order, but by topic. For instance, in a federal code, all the federal statutes relating to interstate highways are placed under one title, all the statutes relating to veterans' benefits are placed under a different title, and all the statutes relating to Social Security benefits are placed under yet another title. The decision about where to place a particular statute is made not by Congress itself but by attorneys who work for the Office of the Law Revision Counsel.

The unannotated code for federal statutes is the *United States Code* (U.S.C.). It is published by the United States Printing Office, and it is the official version of the United States statutes. You can find the *United States Code* in book form in most law libraries and larger public libraries. In addition, you can also find free copies on a number of websites, including the following:

http://www.loc.gov/law/help/guide/federal/uscode.php
http://uscode.house.gov
www.gpoaccess.gov/uscode/index.html
http://lp.findlaw.com

Use an unannotated code when all you need is the text of the particular statute or when you want to see several different sections.

c. Annotated Codes

An annotated code is a code that contains not only the text of the statutes but also historical notes, cross-references to other sources published by the same publisher, and Notes of Decisions/Case Notes. Thus, an annotated code is both a primary authority because it sets out the law itself and a finding tool because you can use it to find other primary and secondary authorities.

For federal statutes, there are two annotated codes. *The United States Code Annotated* (U.S.C.A.) is published by West, a Thomson Reuters business, and is available both in books and on Westlaw Classic and WestlawNext. The *United States Code Service* (U.S.C.S.) is published by LexisNexis and is available both in books and on Lexis.com and Lexis Advance. You should use an annotated code when you are interested not only in the text of the statute but also in how the courts have interpreted and applied the statute.

| **PRACTICE POINTER** | All your citations to federal statutes should be to the U.S.C. and not to the U.S.C.A. or the U.S.C.S. Cite to the U.S.C.A. or the U.S.C.S. only when the material appears in one of those sources but not in |

the U.S.C. See Rule 14.1 in the *ALWD Citation Manual* and Rule 12.2.1 in *The Bluebook*.

| **Exercise 5B** | **Federal Statutes** |

For this exercise, select one of the following statutory sections:

a. 17 U.S.C. § 1201 (2012)
b. 18 U.S.C. § 228 (2012)
c. 12 U.S.C. § 1811 (2012)

Locate the text of your statutory section in each of the following:

1. The book version of the *United States Code*
2. The book version of the *United States Code Annotated*
3. The book version of the *United States Code Service*
4. http://law.justia.com/us/codes/
5. Lexis Advance or WestlawNext

Is the text of the statute the same in each source? In each source, what types of information are set out after the text of the statute?

---

d. Federal Regulations

In enacting a statute, Congress often grants an administrative agency the power to promulgate regulations. When agencies follow the proper procedures for promulgating these regulations, the regulations have the effect of law and are, therefore, primary authority.

For most agencies, the procedures for promulgating regulations are set out in the Administrative Procedure Act. This Act, which is codified at 5 U.S.C. § 551 and the sections that follow, require (1) that notice of a proposed regulation be published in the *Federal Register*, (2) that there be time for comment and hearings, and (3) that the final version of the regulation be published initially in the *Federal Register* and permanently in the *Code of Federal Regulations*.

You can find the book version of the *Code of Federal Regulations* (C.F.R.) in most law libraries and in larger public libraries. In addition, you can find copies of the C.F.R. on a number of free websites. For instance, you can find the entire text of the C.F.R. on the Government Printing Office's website, *http://www.gpoaccess.gov/cfr*, and on FindLaw for Professionals, *http://lp.findlaw.com*. You can also find selected C.F.R. sections on agency websites. For example, you can find the regulations that relate to the Social Security Act on the Social Security Administration's website (*http://ssa.gov/regulations*), and you can find the regulations that relate to U.S. national parks on the National Park Service's website (*http://home.nps.gov/applications/npspolicy/getregs.cfm*).

There are also a number of sites that provide access to all or part of the *Federal Register*. You can find the complete text of the *Federal Register* on the Government Printing Office's website, www.gpoaccess.gov/fr and on www.regulations.gov, which not only lists proposed regulations but also provides a vehicle for commenting on those proposed regulations. Another site that can be used to comment on proposed regulations is http://www.regulations.gov/#!home.

To find regulations that have been promulgated pursuant to a particular section of the *United States Code*, use one of the tables that provides cross-references. See, for example, see the tables that are available at *http://www.gpo.gov/help/parallel_table.pdf*.

Exercise 5C   **Federal Regulations**

For this exercise, select one of the following regulations:

a. 25 C.F.R. § 309.1
b. 34 C.F.R. § 636.10
c. 45 C.F.R. § 144.101

Locate your statutory section in each of the following sources:

1. *Code of Federal Regulations*
2. *www.gpoaccess.gov/cfr/*
3. Lexis.com, Lexis Advance, Westlaw Classic, or WestlawNext

For each source, briefly summarize the types of information that you find. Does each source set out the same information? If not, describe the types of information in each source.

---

§ 5.2.3   Sources for Cases That Have Interpreted or Applied a Federal Statute or Regulation

a.   Finding Tools

When the statute and any applicable regulations answer your question, you do not need to look for cases that have interpreted or applied that statute.

However, when the statute and its applicable regulations are ambiguous, you do. One of the easiest ways to find these cases is to use the Notes of Decisions/Case Notes following the statutory section.

PRACTICE POINTER	Not all statutes have corresponding regulations. For example, there are no regulations for criminal statutes.

As soon as they issue a decision, the federal courts send an electronic copy of the decision to the publishing companies (for example, LexisNexis and Thomson West), and these companies create a Note of Decision or Case Note of each point of law addressed in the decision. In addition to placing these "summaries" as headnotes at the beginning of the case, if the summary relates to a particular statute, the publishing company places that summary after the text of the statute.

If there are relatively few cases that have discussed a particular statute, the Notes of Decisions/Case Notes will be listed by court and date after the statute. (Notes of Decisions/Case Notes from higher courts will be listed before Notes of Decisions/Case Notes from lower courts, and Notes of Decisions/Case Notes from more recent cases will be listed before Notes of Decisions/Case Notes from older cases.) If, however, there are a number of cases that have discussed a particular statute, the Notes of Decisions/Case Notes will be organized by subtopics and then, within those topics, by court and date. Your job as a legal researcher is to select the topics that appear to be on point and then to read through the Notes of Decisions/Case Notes under those topics, identifying the cases that appear to be most on point. Once you identify the cases that appear to be most on point, locate and read the relevant portions of those cases.

PRACTICE POINTER	Because the Notes of Decisions/Case Notes are created by the publishing companies, the notes are finding tools and are not something you can cite to in a memo or a brief.

You can also find cases using the citations that you found during the course of your background reading, by using a federal digest or by doing a search on Lexis.com, Lexis Advance, Westlaw Classic, WestlawNext, Bloomberg Law, or a free Internet site.

Exercise 5D   Notes of Decisions/Case Notes

1. Using the book version of the *United States Code Annotated,* find the most recent case listed under 29 U.S.C. § 2611 that has discussed the length of employment requirements. Record the name and citation for the case.
2. Using Lexis Advance and WestlawNext, find the most recent case listed under 29 U.S.C. § 2611 that has discussed the length of employment/requisite hours of service requirements. Is the case that you found using the book version of the *United States Code Annotated* the same case that you found using Lexis Advance and WestlawNext? If it isn't, why did you find different cases?

b. Reporters

Federal cases are published in a number of reporters, which are sets of books that publish the text of court decisions, not by topic, but in the order in which the cases were decided. Table 5.2 shows the reporters in which decisions from the United States Supreme Court, the United States Courts of Appeals, and the United States District Courts are published.

Table 5.2	List of Federal Reporters		
COURT	**NAME OF REPORTER**	**ABBREVIATION**	**COVERAGE DATES**
United States Supreme Court (appellate court)	*United States Reports*	U.S.	1789 to date
	Supreme Court Reporter	S. Ct.	1882 to date
	United States Supreme Court Reports, Lawyers' Edition	L. Ed.	1879 to 1956
	United States Supreme Court Reports, Lawyers' Edition, Second Series	L. Ed. 2d	1956 to date
United States Courts of Appeals (appellate court)	*Federal Reporter*	F.	1889 to 1924
	Federal Reporter, Second Series	F.2d	1924 to 1993
	Federal Reporter, Third Series	F.3d	1993 to date
United States District Courts (trial court)	*Federal Supplement*	F. Supp.	1932 to 1998
	Federal Supplement, Second Series	F. Supp. 2d	1998 to date
	Federal Rules Decisions (contains district court decisions interpreting and applying the Federal Rules of Civil Procedure)	F.R.D.	1938 to date

PRACTICE POINTER Although all United States Supreme Court opinions are reported, or published, not all United States District Court and United States Court of Appeals opinions are reported in the book versions of the official federal reporters. While historically you could not cite unreported cases, that rule changed in 2006 when the United States Supreme Court announced that unpublished opinions decided after January 1, 2007, could be cited. See Federal Rule of Appellate Procedure 32.1, available at *http://www.law.cornell.edu/rules/frap/rules.html.*

To find a federal case in a book or electronic source, use the case cita-tion. In particular, use the volume number, the abbreviation for the reporter, and the page number. Look for a moment at the following citation, which is the full citation for the United States Supreme Court's decision in *Brown v. Board of Education*.

> *Brown v. Board of Education*, 347 U.S. 483, 74 S. Ct. 686, 98 L. Ed. 873 (1954).

This citation tells you that you can find a copy of the Court's decision in *Brown v. Board of Education* in three different reporters: volume 347 of the *United States Reports* beginning on page 483; volume 74 of the *Supreme Court Reporter* beginning on page 686; and volume 98 of the *United States Supreme Court Reports, Lawyers' Edition*, beginning on page 873. The first citation, the citation to the *United States Reports*, is the official citation. The citations to the *Supreme Court Reporter* and the *United States Supreme Court Reports, Lawyers' Edition*, are parallel citations. For more on reading citations, see Chapter 3.

Both the *Supreme Court Reporter* and the *United States Supreme Court Reports, Lawyers' Edition*, are unofficial reporters published by private publish-ing companies. (The *Supreme Court Reporter* is published by West, a Thomson Reuters business, and the *United States Supreme Court Reports, Lawyers' Edition*, is published by LexisNexis.) While the text of the opinion will be the same in all three reporters, the headnotes and other editorial enhancements will be different.

Although some law firms have their state reporters in book form, fewer have the book versions of the federal reporters. As a consequence, to find the text of a federal case, you will usually have to use an online source. You can do so using a fee-based service, such as Lexis Advance or WestlawNext, or on a free website. For example, most federal cases are now on Google® Scholar.

Exercise 5E	**Sources for United States Supreme Court Decisions**

Locate the text of *Bush v. Gore*, 531 U.S. 98, 121 S. Ct. 525, 148 L. Ed. 2d 388 (2000), in each of the following sources:

a. The *United States Reports* (U.S.).
b. The *Supreme Court Reporter* (S. Ct.)
c. The *United States Supreme Court Reports, Lawyers' Edition, Second Series* (L. Ed. 2d)
d. Google Scholar
e. *http://www.supremecourtus.gov/opinions/opinions.html*

For each of the sources above, answer the following questions:

1. Is there a "summary" or "syllabus" before the text of the opinion?
2. Are there headnotes?
3. Are the summaries and headnotes the same in each source? If they are not the same, why aren't they the same?

§ 5.2.4 Sources for Additional Secondary Authority

a. Law Reviews and Law Journals

Law reviews and law journals publish articles about the law. Some of these journals are general in nature, publishing articles on a wide range of topics. (See, for example, the *Maine Law Review* and the *Stanford Law Review*.) Others deal with specific areas of the law, for instance, environmental law or international law. (See, for example, *Journal of Environmental Law and Litigation* and *Harvard International Law Journal*.) In addition, some organizations and groups also publish law reviews. While most law review articles are written by law school professors, law reviews also publish articles written by judges and practitioners, and notes and comments written by law students.

Use law reviews when you are looking for information about a new area of law or a new issue in an established area of law. You can find law review articles in the book version of the individual law reviews themselves and online on Lexis.com, Lexis Advance, Westlaw Classic, or WestlawNext. In addition, a few law schools have begun putting their law reviews on their websites, and some journals are available for free. See the American Bar Association's website (*http://www.americanbar.org/groups/departments_offices/legal_technology_resources/resources/free_journal_search.html*), SSRN (*http://papers.ssrn.com/sol3/DisplayAbstractSearch.cfm*), or Google Scholar (*http://scholar.google.com/schhp?hl=en&as_sdt=0,48*).

b. *American Law Reports,* Federal

American Law Reports (A.L.R.) was first published in 1919 to compete with West's National Reporter System. However, unlike West's National Reporter System, which publishes every reported state and federal decision, A.L.R. is selective, publishing only "significant" cases and annotations that discuss the issues raised in those cases. These annotations, which are researched and written by attorneys, collect and summarize cases that have discussed a particular issue. The annotations that deal with federal issues are set out in A.L.R. Fed. and A.L.R. Fed. 2d.

You can find the A.L.R. in your law library or online on Lexis.com, Lexis Advance, Westlaw Classic, or WestlawNext. In the book, you can find annotations using the subject index; online, you can find annotations using a terms and connectors search or doing a natural language search.

c. Looseleaf Services

Historically, looseleaf services were what their name suggests: a service that provided information in "looseleaf" notebooks, which were updated by taking out a page and replacing that page with a new page. Today, most looseleaf services are available both in book form and on fee-based services such as Lexis.com, Lexis Advance, Westlaw Classic, or WestlawNext.

Although each looseleaf service is different, most deal with specialized areas of law: There are looseleaf services that deal with federal tax issues, with federal benefits issues (for example, Social Security), and with other federal issues (for example, environmental issues). Most looseleaf services provide a wide range of up-to-date information about these specialized areas. For example, many of them provide the text of the applicable statutes and regulations, the text of proposed legislation and regulations, and summaries of relevant court and administrative decisions.

To determine which looseleaf services are in your library, check your library's electronic card catalog or ask a law librarian. To determine which looseleaf services are available on a particular fee-based service, check the service's database directory or ask your service's representative.

PRACTICE POINTER	Because looseleaf services are expensive, they may not be included in the basic Lexis.com, Lexis Advance, Westlaw Classic, or WestlawNext service package. You can, however, access them for an additional fee.

Exercise 5F   Sources for Law Review Articles

Locate one of the following law review articles both in book form in the library and on either Lexis Advance or WestlawNext:

1. John B. Kirkwood, The Robinson-Patman Act and Consumer Welfare: Has Volvo Reconciled Them? 30 Seattle U. L. Rev. 349 (2007).
2. Lorraine K. Bannai, Taking the Stand: The Lessons of Three Men Who Took the Japanese American Internment to Court, 4 Seattle J. Soc. Just. 1 (2005).
3. Michael Ashley Stein, Same Struggle, Different Difference: ADA Accommodations as Antidiscrimination, 153 U. Pa. L. Rev. 579 (2004).

Copy the first page of the print version, and print out the first page from Lexis.com, Lexis Advance, Westlaw Classic, or WestlawNext.

§ 5.3   Using the Research Plan to Research an Issue Governed by Federal Statutes and Regulations

To research issues governed by federal statutes and regulations, you have a number of options: You can research the issue using books; fee-based services like Westlaw Classic, WestlawNext, Lexis.com, Lexis Advance, Bloomberg Law; or free websites. While in practice you will seldom use a single tool, in this section we walk you through the process of researching an issue governed by federal statutes and regulations in six ways. While you do not need to go through each section, do go through several, comparing and contrasting the advantages and disadvantages of each.

To learn more about using free and fee-based services to research issues governed by federal statutes or regulations, see the electronic supplement.

PRACTICE POINTER
You should be able to do most statutory research using free sources: State and federal statutes are available on free government websites that are both reliable and up-to-date. In addition, you can find the text of cases that have cited a statute using free websites, for instance, the "Selected courts" options on Google Scholar. You may, though, want to use an annotated code to find cases, which means that you will need to use Lexis Advance, WestlawNext, Lexis.com, or Westlaw Classic. (At this point, Bloomberg Law does not have an annotated code.) In addition, you will need to cite check any cases that you use using *Shepard's*®, KeyCite®, or BCite, which is on Bloomberg Law.

§ 5.3.1   The Assignment
§ 5.3.2   Researching an Issue Governed by Federal Statutes and Regulations Using Free Websites
§ 5.3.3   Researching an Issue Governed by Federal Statutes and Regulations Using Lexis Advance
§ 5.3.4   Researching an Issue Governed by Federal Statutes and Regulations Using WestlawNext
§ 5.3.5   Researching an Issue Governed by Federal Statutes and Regulations using Bloomberg Law
§ 5.3.6   Researching an Issue Governed by Federal Statutes and Regulations Using Lexis.com
§ 5.3.7   Researching an Issue Governed by Federal Statutes and Regulations Using Westlaw Classic

Chapter 5 Quiz

Draft answers for each of the following questions. Make your points clearly and concisely, and write sentences that are easy to read and that are grammatical and correctly punctuated.

1. As a general rule, where is the best place to do background reading about a federal statute? For example, where would be the best place to do background reading on disability benefits under the Social Security Act?

2. How is the organizational scheme that is used in the *Statutes at Large* different from the organizational scheme that is used in the *United States Code*?

3. What is the difference between an unannotated code and an annotated code?

4. When would you cite to the *United States Code Annotated*?

5. How can you determine whether there are federal regulations that relate to a particular section of the *United States Code*?

6. What is a Note of Decision? A Case Note?

7. What is a reporter?

8. What is a parallel cite?

9. Where can you find a free copy of United States District Court decisions?

10. What type of information is in A.L.R. Fed. 2d?

Researching Issues Governed by City or County Ordinances

I f you are like many law students, when you applied to law school you envisioned yourself working on the big issues: prosecuting or defending individuals charged with felonies, investigating major corporate scandals, or working to enforce treaties protecting the environment or basic human rights.

Although you may end up working on high-profile cases or issues of national or international importance, it is also likely that you will work on smaller, more local cases, cases that are governed not by federal or state statutes or international treaties but by city or county ordinances. While these cases may not make the front page of anything other than your local newspaper, they involve important issues. For it is often city or county ordinances that determine what can and cannot be built in our neighborhoods, what our local businesses can and cannot do, and what does and does not constitute a nuisance.

Like Chapters 4 and 5, this chapter has several components: (1) the text, which sets out basic information; (2) exercises, which ask you to apply what you have just read; (3) a quiz that tests the materials set out in the chapter; and (4) an electronic supplement, which shows you how to research an issue governed by local law using free sources, Lexis Advance®, WestlawNext™, Bloomberg Law, Lexis.com®, and Westlaw® Classic. To access the supplement, go to *http://www.aspenlawschool.com/books/oates_legalwritinghandbook/*. Your access code to the website is on the card that came with the book. In the ebook, instructions for getting an access code are on the page immediately following the cover page.

§ 6.1   An Introduction to City and County Government

In many ways, city and county governments are analogous to state governments. Just as the state constitutions define a state's powers and responsibilities, charters define a county's or city's powers and responsibilities. In addition, just as the federal and state governments have three branches, so do counties and cities. Cities and counties have a legislative branch (for example, a city or county council) that enacts legislation; an executive branch (for example, a county executive, mayor, or city manager) that enforces that legislation; and a court system (for example, a district or municipal court) that has limited jurisdiction.

§ 6.2   Research Plans for Issues Governed by City or County Ordinances

Because many cases involving city or county ordinances involve small amounts of money or are brought by individuals with limited resources, you will often need to research issues involving ordinances quickly and inexpensively. Accordingly, the first research plan is designed to help you answer relatively simple questions in just an hour or two, using free sources. There will, of course, be other cases in which you need to do more thorough research. The second research plan is designed to help you research those issues.

Plan No. 1:

Research Plan for Quickly and Inexpensively Researching an Issue Governed by a City or County Ordinance

Jurisdiction: [Enter the name of the city or county.]

Type of Law: Enacted law

**Preliminary Issue
Statement:**   [Put your first draft of the issue statement here.]

Step 1:   Locate your city or county ordinances on the city or county website or on a free website that provides links to city and county websites, for example, *http://www.municode.com* or *http://www.statelocalgov.net*.

Step 2:   Read and analyze the applicable section or sections and then apply the plain language of those sections to the facts of your case.

Plan No. 2:

Research Plan for Doing More Thorough Research of an Issue Governed by a City or County Ordinance

Jurisdiction: [Enter the name of the city or county.]

Type of Law: Enacted law

Preliminary Issue

Statement: [Put your first draft of the issue statement here.]

Step 1:   Locate your city or county ordinances on the city or county website or on a free website that provides links to city and county websites, for example, *http://www.municode.com* or *http://www.statelocalgov.net.*

Step 2:   Read and analyze the applicable sections, determining whether the ordinance is constitutional and identifying the elements and determining which elements appear to be in dispute. If none of the elements is likely to be in dispute, stop researching. If, however, one or more of the elements are likely to be in dispute, research the disputed elements using Steps 3–6.

Step 3:   Using free websites, look for articles that discuss the area of law. Using those articles, identify cases that may be on point.

Step 4:   Using free websites, for example, Google® Scholar, or fee-based sites such as Lexis.com, Lexis Advance, Westlaw Classic, or WestlawNext, locate copies of cases that are on point.

Step 5:   Before deciding to use a case, cite check the case to determine (1) whether the case is still good law and (2) whether there are any additional cases that discuss the same point. Look up and, if appropriate, cite check any additional cases you locate.

Step 6:   If appropriate, locate law review articles and other commentaries that might be on point.

§ 6.3   Sources for Researching Issues Governed by City or Ordinances

In researching issues governed by city or county ordinances, you will usually be looking for one or more of the following documents.

§ 6.3.1   Charters

In most instances, you will not need to find a copy of the city or county charter. For example, you will not need to find a copy of the charter when common sense tells you that the city or county had the power to enact a particular ordinance or do a particular act.

However, when you do need to find a copy of the charter, look first on the city or county website. To do this, use a search engine such as Bing or Google, and type in the name of the city, the name of the state, and the word "charter." In the alternative, look for a website that collects and publishes charters for the counties or cities in your state, or contact your county or city offices and ask the clerk to email you an electronic copy of the charter.

Exercise 6A	City Charters

Find the city charter for one of the following cities using Bing or Google. Record the URL for the page that contains a copy of the charter.

   a. San Diego, California
   b. Tampa, Florida
   c. Seattle, Washington
   d. Bangor, Maine
   e. The city in which your law school is located

§ 6.3.2   Ordinances

Charters give cities and counties the power to enact certain types of legislation. For example, as a general rule, cities and counties have the power to enact legislation governing activities such as the use of property, the operation of businesses, and the creation and governance of parks when these activities are within the city's or county's boundaries. These pieces of legislation, which are similar to statutes, are called ordinances. Like state and federal statutes, ordinances are enacted by the legislative branch (for example, the city council) and enforced by the executive branch (for example, the city agencies and the city police).

Many cities and counties post copies of their ordinances on their official city or county websites. In addition, some free websites collect or provide links to city and county ordinances—for example, *http://www.statelocalgov .net* and *http://www.municode.com*. As a last resort, you can usually obtain a paper copy of the ordinances from either the city or county clerk or at the local public library.

Because not all counties and cities update their materials regularly, always check to make sure the ordinances you find are the ordinances that govern. If the cause of action arose in the past, make sure you have the ordinances that were in effect at the time the cause of action arose. In contrast, if you are advising a client about what it can or cannot do in the future, make sure you know what the ordinances currently say and what changes have been proposed.

Exercise 6B	Municipal Ordinances

Find the municipal ordinances for one of the following cities using Bing or Google. Record the URL for the page that contains a copy of the ordinances.

   a. San Diego, California
   b. Tampa, Florida
   c. Seattle, Washington
   d. Bangor, Maine
   e. Your city

§ 6.3.3   Other City or County Documents

Sometimes you will need to find copies of other city or county documents. For example, you may want to find the minutes of a city or county council meeting to find out what the council intended when it adopted a particular ordinance; you may want to find the decisions of a city or county commission, department, or agency; or you might want to find a record that was filed with a city or county. Although you may be able to find some of this information on the city's, county's, commission's, or department's website, more likely than not you will have to obtain that information from the city or county itself.

§ 6.4   Using the Research Plan to Research an Issue Governed by City or County Ordinances

To research issues governed by city or county ordinances, you have a number of options: You can research the issue using books and fee-based services such as WestlawNext, Lexis Advance, or Bloomberg Law. However, in almost all instances, the best option is free websites.

To learn more about using free and fee-based services to research issues governed by city or county ordinances, see the electronic supplement, especially section 6.4.2.

§ 6.4.1   The Assignment

§ 6.4.2   Researching an Issue Governed by City or County Ordinances Using Free Websites

§ 6.4.3   Researching an Issue Governed by City or County Ordinances Using Lexis Advance

§ 6.4.4   Researching an Issue Governed by City or County Ordinances Using WestlawNext

§ 6.4.5   Researching an Issue Governed by City or County Ordinances Using Bloomberg Law

§ 6.4.6   Researching an Issue Governed by City or County Ordinances Using Lexis.com

§ 6.4.7   Researching an Issue Governed by City or County Ordinances Using Westlaw Classic

Chapter 6 Quiz

Draft answers for each of the following questions. Make your points clearly and concisely, and write sentences that are easy to read and that are grammatical and correctly punctuated.

1. What function(s) does a city charter serve?
2. Where can you find a copy of a city's or county's charter?
3. What is an ordinance?
4. Where can you find a copy of city ordinances that are currently in effect?
5. What entities typically function as the executive and legislative branches of a city or county?

Researching Common Law and Constitutional Issues

Researching Issues Governed by Common Law

While common law problems are no longer so common, there are still some issues that are governed by common law. As a result, you need to know how to find the cases that set out and apply common law rules.

Like the prior chapters, this chapter has several components: (1) the text, which sets out basic information; (2) exercises, which ask you to apply what you have just read; (3) a quiz that tests the materials set out in the chapter; and (4) and electronic supplement, which shows you how to research an issue governed by common law using free sources, Lexis Advance®, WestlawNext™, Bloomberg Law, Lexis.com®, and Westlaw® Classic. To access the supplement, go to *http://www.aspenlawschool.com/books/oates_legalwriting handbook/*. Your access code to the website is on the card that came with the book. In the ebook, instructions for getting an access code are on the page immediately following the cover page.

§ 7.1   Are All Cases the Same?

The answer to this question is no. In fact, cases fall into two categories. In one category are the cases that set out, interpret, and apply the common law, and in the other category are the cases that interpret and apply enacted law.

The following example shows how common law rules are created and the relationship between common law rules, enacted law, and the cases that interpret and apply enacted law.

Assume for the moment a blank slate. You are in a state with no common law rules and no statutes, ordinances, or regulations. The first case that your state's courts hear is *In re Marriage of Adamson*.

In *Adamson*, a mother asks the court to grant her custody of her two children, a 2-year-old son and a 4-year-old daughter. Because the slate is blank, the court must make its own law. After considering the community's norms and the facts of the case, the court grants the mother's request for custody on the grounds that young children should be with their mother.

Not long after the court decides *Adamson*, another mother requests custody of her children, a 4-year-old son and a 14-year-old daughter. Unlike the situation in *Adamson*, in this situation the slate is not blank. There is now precedent. In deciding *Brown*, the court will be guided by the court's decision in *Adamson*. The reasoning in *Adamson* (that young children should be with their mother) is now a common law rule that the court applies in *Brown*.

Applying that common law rule, the court grants the mother custody of her 4-year-old son. There is, however, no rule that deals with 14-year-old daughters. Consequently, the court is once again in the position of creating a common law rule. This time, the court rules that teenage daughters should remain with their mother and grants the mother custody of her daughter.

In the next case, *In re Marriage of Carey*, a mother with a history of abusing alcohol asks the court to grant her custody of her two daughters, who are 5 and 13. In deciding this case, the court applies both the common law rule set out in *Adamson* — that young children should be with their mother — and the common law rule set out in *Brown* — that teenage daughters should remain with their mother — and grants the mother custody of both daughters. In granting the mother custody, the court interprets the rules set out in *Adamson* and *Brown*, deciding that those common law rules apply even if the mother has a history of abusing alcohol.

As *Adamson*, *Brown*, and *Carey* illustrate, in a common law system, the court's reasoning in one case becomes a common law rule that is applied in the next case. Of course, not all the rules announced in earlier cases are applied in all subsequent cases. For instance, if Case 4, *In re Marriage of Davidson*, involves the custody of a 1-year-old girl whose mother does not have a history of alcohol abuse, the court would apply only the rule announced in *Adamson*; it would not need to consider the additional common law rules set out in *Brown* and *Carey*. Nor does each case need to add to the existing law. The court could decide *Davidson* without creating any new rules.

Continuing with our example, presume that a few years after the court decided *In re Marriage of Davidson*, the legislature enacts a statute that sets out the rules for determining child custody issues. In enacting this statute, the legislature can do one of two things: It can enact or "codify" the common law rule, or it can abolish the common law rule and create its own statute-based rule. If the legislature enacts or codifies the common law rule, the cases that were decided before the statute was enacted are still good law, and the courts can use them in deciding how to interpret and apply the statute. If, however, the legislature abolishes the common law rule, the cases that were decided before the statute was enacted are, most likely, no longer good law.

In our example, the legislature decides to abolish the common law rules that favor awarding custody to the mother. Under the statute, the courts must grant custody "in accordance with the best interests of the children." In determining what is in the best interests of the children, the courts must consider a variety of factors including "the parents' wishes; the children's wishes; the interaction and inter-relationship of the child with parents and siblings; the child's adjustment to his or her home, school, and community; and the mental and physical health of all of the individuals involved." Because this statute abolished the common law rules set out in *Adamson, Brown,* and *Carey,* these cases are, to the extent that they are inconsistent with the statute, no longer good law. Accordingly, when Case 5, *In re Marriage of Edwards,* comes before the court, the court applies the statute and not the rules from *Adamson, Brown,* and *Carey.*

The application of a statute is not, however, always clear. For example, assume that in *Edwards,* the mother contends that she should be given custody, not because the children are young, but because she has always been their primary caregiver. Although the statute does not specifically address this argument, the court agrees with the mother, reasoning that because the mother has always been the primary caregiver, it would be in the children's best interest to remain with her.

Because the court's reasoning in *Edwards* (that it is in the best interests of the children to remain with the parent who has been their primary care-giver) is not inconsistent with the statute, that reasoning can be used by the courts in subsequent cases. In deciding Case 6, *In re Marriage of Forino,* the court will apply not just the statute, but also the reasoning announced in *Edwards.* Similarly, in deciding Case 7, *In re Marriage of Gonzales,* the court will consider not only the statute and the reasoning from *Edwards,* but also the reasoning from *Forino.* Although the "rules" created in *Edwards* and *Forino* create precedent, these cases do not, at least technically, fall into the category of cases that we call the common law. Instead, they fall into a second category: They are simply cases that interpret and apply enacted law.

§ 7.2   Modifying the Generic Research Plan for Issues That Are Governed by Common Law

Before electronic research became common, the tools that attorneys used to research issues governed by state and federal statutes were very different from the tools that they used to research common law issues. When they researched an issue that was governed by a statute, attorneys used an annotated code to find the cases that had interpreted and applied the statute. (See Chapters 4 and 5.) In contrast, when they researched a common law issue, attorneys used a digest to find both the common law rule and the cases that had interpreted and applied that common law rule. While digests are still an excellent finding tool, today many lawyers use fee-based services such as Lexis Advance, WestlawNext and Bloomberg Law or free Internet sites to find the cases setting out and applying common law doctrines.

Research Plan for an Issue Governed by Common Law

Jurisdiction: [Enter the name of the applicable state.]

Type of Law: Common law

Preliminary Issue
Statement: [Put your first draft of the issue statement here.]

Step 1:   If you are unfamiliar with the area of law, spend thirty to sixty minutes doing background reading on the Internet, in a state practice manual or book, a hornbook or *Nutshell*, or a legal encyclopedia.

Step 2:   Locate the cases from your jurisdiction that set out and apply the common law rules.

Step 3:   Cite check the cases that you plan to use to make sure that they are still good law.

Step 4:   If appropriate, locate cases from other jurisdictions, law review articles, or other commentaries that might be on point.

§ 7.3   Sources for Researching Problems Governed by State Common Law

Table 7.1 lists some, but not all, of the sources you can use in researching an issue governed by common law. Because the names of the sources vary by state, we have listed the sources using generic labels and not specific names. You can, however, find the names of your state's practice books using your library's electronic card catalog, and you can find the names of your state's reporters using Appendix 1 of the *ALWD Citation Manual* or Table 1 in *The Bluebook*. Finally, note that not all states will have all the sources listed.

§ 7.3.1   Background Reading

a.   The Internet

As you learned in Chapter 5, sometimes you can do your background reading on the Internet. For example, in some states, there are law firms that post plain language explanations of common law doctrines. One of the easiest ways to find these types of websites is to use Bing or Google, or another search engine. Simply type in the name of your state and terms that describe the doctrine. Remember, though, that information on free websites may not be accurate or up-to-date. Accordingly, use the websites to familiarize yourself with the doctrine but not as authority.

b.   Practice Manuals and Books

Although sometimes you can find good information about a common law doctrine on a free website, most of the time the best source is a state practice

Table 7.1	**State Law Research Tools**
	State Law
Background Reading	• The Internet • State practice manuals and practice books • Hornbooks • *Nutshells* • Legal encyclopedias
Finding Tools	• State practice manuals and practice books • State digests • Regional digests • Fee-based services, such as Lexis.com, Lexis Advance, Westlaw Classic, and WestlawNext • Free websites such as Google Scholar, FindLaw, Justia.com, lexisONE®, or a state government website
Cases	• State reporter containing decisions from the state's highest appellate court • State reporter containing decisions from the state's intermediate appellate court • West regional reporter containing decisions from the state's highest appellate court and the state's intermediate appellate court • Fee-based services, such as Lexis.com, Lexis Advance, Westlaw Classic, and WestlawNext • Free websites, such as Google Scholar, FindLaw, Justia.com, lexisONE, or a state government website
Cite Checking	• KeyCite • *Shepard's* • BCite
Secondary Authorities	• *American Law Reports* (for example, A.L.R.4th, A.L.R.5th, and A.L.R.6th) • Law review articles

manual or book. These manuals usually provide a short history of the common law rule or doctrine, the general rules, and citations to key cases. In addition, if there are any statutes that affect the common law doctrine, the manuals usually provide you with cross-references to those statutes. Some examples of state practice manuals are *Trawick's Florida Practice and Procedure, Illinois Law and Practice,* and *Washington Practice.* While some practice books are available only in book form, increasingly they are being added to fee-based services. For instance, the Thomson West practice books are on Westlaw Classic and WestlawNext, and many state bar publications are on Loislaw.

c.   Hornbooks and *Nutshells*

Hornbooks and *Nutshells* are also a good source for background reading. Like practice manuals, these books provide you with a short history of the common law rule and with the general rules. In addition, they usually include descriptions and citations to cases. However, unlike a state practice manual, which lists cases from a single state, hornbooks set out citations to cases from a variety of states.

Most hornbooks are available only in book form. To find them in your library, use your library's electronic card catalog or ask a librarian.

d.   Legal Encyclopedias

If one is available, you can also do background reading in a legal encyclopedia. While a few states have their own legal encyclopedia, most states do not. As a result, you will need to use a more general encyclopedia, for example, *American Jurisprudence, Second Series* (Am. Jur. 2d) or *Corpus Juris Secundum* (C.J.S.). You can find legal encyclopedias in book form in your law library or on fee-based services such as Lexis Advance and WestlawNext. In addition, the Legal Information Institute at Cornell Law School sponsors and hosts a free online dictionary and legal encyclopedia. This dictionary and encyclopedia, which is called WEX, is available at *http://www.law.cornell.edu/wex/*.

Exercise 7A   **Background Reading**

1. Using your law school's electronic card catalog, locate a hornbook that discusses adverse possession. Record the name of the hornbook, its call number, and the chapter or sections that discuss adverse possession.
2. Does WEX, the free online dictionary and legal encyclopedia sponsored and hosted by the Legal Information Institute at Cornell Law School, discuss adverse possession? See *http://www.law .cornell.edu/wex/*. If yes, is the information helpful? Why or why not?
3. Using Bing or Google, look for websites that provide an overview of the law relating to adverse possession. What are the pros and cons of using free Internet sites?

---

§ 7.3.2   Finding Tools

While at one point digests were the best way to find cases setting out and applying common law rules, today there are a number of other good ways to find cases.

a.   Practice Manuals and Books

If you do your background reading in a practice manual or book, you can use that practice manual to find cases. More likely than not, the practice manual will cite cases that set out the common law rule and explain who has the burden of proof and what that burden is. You can find these cases in a number of ways:

- Use the citation to locate the cases in the book version of a state, regional, or federal reporter;
- Use the citation to find the case on Google® Scholar, Justia.com, or FindLaw®;
- Use the "Find by citation" option to find the cases on a Lexis.com or Westlaw Classic; or
- Type the citation into the search window on Lexis Advance, WestlawNext, or Bloomberg Law.

b. Digests

Digests are subject indexes for both common law cases and cases that interpret and apply enacted law. Each digest is divided into a number of topics, with those topics divided into subtopics and, sometimes, sub-subtopics. Under these topic headings are Notes of Decisions from cases that have discussed the particular point of law.

West publishes a number of digests, including state digests, which contain headnotes from the cases published in the corresponding state reporters; regional digests, which contain headnotes from the cases published in the corresponding regional reporter; and federal digests, which can be used to find cases published in the *Supreme Court Reporter*, the first, second, and third series of the *Federal Reporter*, and the first and second series of the *Federal Supplement*. In addition, West publishes a number of specialty digests, for example, the *Bankruptcy Digest*, the *Military Justice Digest*, and the *Education Law Digest*.

Digests published by West use the West Key Number System®, which works as follows. Through the years, West has created a series of topics and within those topics, "Key Numbers" for each point of law. This set of topics and Key Numbers is the West Key Number System.

When a court publishes an opinion, it sends a copy of its opinion to West, which assigns the case to an editor. The editor, who is an attorney, identifies each point of law discussed in the court's opinion, writes a single sentence, summarizing that point of law, and then assigns that summary a topic and Key Number. These summaries are used in three ways. First, West uses them as headnotes for the case. Second, if the summary relates to a statute, the summary is placed in the Notes of Decision following the applicable statute. Third, these summaries are placed in the appropriate digests under their assigned topic and Key Number.

> **PRACTICE POINTER** Because the headnotes are written by the company that publishes the reporter and not by the court, you can never cite to a headnote as authority. Instead, you must cite to that part of the court's opinion from which the publishing company took the point of law summarized in the headnote. Similarly, you cannot cite the Notes of Decisions set out following a statute in an annotated code or presented in a digest. Instead, you must read and cite the case from which the Note of Decision was drawn.

c. Fee-Based Services

There are a number of ways to find cases using Lexis.com, Lexis Advance, Westlaw Classic, WestlawNext, and Bloomberg Law. If, during your background reading, you located a case that is on point, you can use that case to find additional cases. For example, if you are using Westlaw Classic or WestlawNext, you can identify the headnotes that are on point and then use either the Key Numbers associated with those cases to do a Key Number search or use the "Most Frequently Cited Cases" option.

In the alternative, you can select your state's case law database (use a database that contains all your state's published decisions) and then construct a Boolean (terms and connectors) search that includes a word or phrase that describes the common law doctrine (for instance, "false imprisonment," "battery," or "nuisance") and a word that the courts are likely to have used in setting out the general rules or burden of proof (for example, "prove," "establish," "elements," or "factors"). Once you have found and analyzed the general rules, you can then run additional searches for cases that have interpreted or applied a specific element or factor. See the electronic supplement for more information about running searches in the particular services.

d.   Free Websites

While historically cases were not available on free websites, most cases are now available on Google Scholar. In addition, you can find cases on FindLaw (*http://lp.findlaw.com*) and Justia.com (*http://www.justia.com*).

Exercise 7B	**Finding Tools**

1. Using your library's electronic card catalog, locate a digest. Which volume contains information about adverse possession? What type of information is in the volume? How is the information organized?
2. Go to Google Scholar and select "Legal Documents" and then, on the next screen, your state's courts. Run a search and note the first ten cases that your search retrieves. Next, go to Lexis Advance, WestlawNext, or Bloomberg Law. Using the various "filters," limit your search to cases from your jurisdiction and then run the same search that you ran on Google Scholar. Does this search retrieve the same ten cases that your Google Scholar search retrieved? Why or why not?

§ 7.3.3   Cases

The cases setting out, interpreting, and applying common law rules are in the same reporters as the cases that interpret and apply enacted law. In publishing a case, neither the courts nor the publishing companies distinguish between the two categories of cases. Instead, all the cases are grouped together, organized not by type of case or by topic but by the date of the decision.

In some states, decisions are published in both the state's reporter or reporters and in a regional reporter. For example, you can find the Virginia Supreme Court's decisions in both *Virginia Reports* (Va.) and in *South Eastern Reporter* (S.E., S.E.2d) and the Virginia Court of Appeals' decisions in both the *Virginia Court of Appeals Reports* (Va. App.) and *South Eastern Reporter* (S.E., S.E.2d). By contrast, in Maine, recent decisions of the Maine Supreme Court are published only in the *Atlantic Reporter* (A. or A.2d). Maine does not have its own official or state reporter.

Exercise 7C	**Reporters**

1. Using Appendix 1 in the *ALWD Citation Manual* or Table 1 in *The Bluebook*, determine the names of reporters for each of the following states. Record the name of the reporter, the types of decisions that are included in the reporter, and the coverage dates.

   a. Indiana
   b. North Dakota
   c. Wisconsin
   d. The state in which your law school is located

2. Locate the reporters for your state's court and select a case from a recent volume. Is there a summary at the beginning of the case? Are there headnotes? If there are headnotes, which publishing company prepared the headnotes?

§ 7.3.4   Other Authorities

Although most of the time you will be able to answer a client's question using your state's cases, occasionally you will need or want to go beyond those cases and look at cases from other states, or see what others have said about the issue that you have been asked to research. For example, you may want to do this additional type of research if your case involves an issue that has not been dealt with in your state, if different divisions within your state's intermediate appellate court have taken different approaches, or if the case is particularly complex or important.

a.   *American Law Reports*

One of the easiest ways to find cases from other states is to use *American Law Reports* (A.L.R.). While originally A.L.R. served as a reporter, today most researchers use it for its annotations. Each annotation deals with a specific topic and lists cases by result and by jurisdiction.

Annotations dealing with state issues are found in A.L.R., A.L.R.2d, A.L.R.3d, A.L.R.4th, A.L.R.5th, and A.L.R.6th. Annotations dealing with federal issues are found in A.L.R. Fed. or A.L.R. Fed. 2d.

A.L.R.	1919-1948
A.L.R.2d	1948-1965
A.L.R.3d	1965-1980
A.L.R.4th	1980-1991
A.L.R.5th	1992-2005
A.L.R.6th	2005 to present
A.L.R. Fed.	1969-2005
A.L.R. Fed. 2d	2005 to present

A.L.R. is available both in book form and on Lexis.com, Lexis Advance, Westlaw Classic, and WestlawNext. Both the book and the electronic versions have indexes.

> **PRACTICE POINTER**   Because you want the most current information, look first for annotations published in A.L.R.5th, A.L.R.6th, and A.L.R. Fed. 2d. In addition, if you are using the book version, be sure to check the pocket parts for more recent cases.

b. Law Reviews and Journals

If you are looking for an in-depth discussion of a particular common law issue or for a critique of a case that has set out, interpreted, or applied a common law rule, consider looking for a law review article. While most law reviews and journals are published by law schools, some are published by organizations.

You can now access some law review articles for free. For a list of law reviews that are currently available, see *http://www.americanbar.org/groups/depart ments_offices/legal_technology_resources/resources/free_journal_search.html*. In addition, you can find articles using Google Scholar and SSRN.com. Law review articles are also available on Lexis.com, Lexis Advance, Westlaw Classic, and WestlawNext.

§ 7.4   Using the Research Plan to Research an Issue Governed by Common Law

To research issues governed by common law, you have a number of options: You can research the issue using books, free sources, and fee-based services such as Lexis Advance, WestlawNext, and Bloomberg Law. While you do not need to master all of the ways in which you can research common law problems, you should learn to use a number of different tools.

To learn more about using free and fee-based services to research issues governed by common law, see the electronic supplement at *http://www.aspen lawschool.com/books/oates_legalwritinghandbook/*.

§ 7.4.1   The Assignment
§ 7.4.2   Researching an Issue Governed by Common Law Using Free Websites
§ 7.4.3   Researching an Issue Governed by Common Law Using Lexis Advance
§ 7.4.4   Researching an Issue Governed by Common Law Using WestlawNext
§ 7.4.5   Researching an Issue Governed by Common Law Using Bloomberg Law
§ 7.4.6   Researching an Issue Governed by Common Law Using Lexis .com
§ 7.4.7   Researching an Issue Governed by Common Law Using Westlaw Classic

Chapter 7 Quiz

Draft answers for each of the following questions. Make your points clearly and concisely, and write sentences that are easy to read and that are grammatical and correctly punctuated.

1. You have been asked to research a common law issue that involves an area of law that you did not study in law school. Where should you start your research?
2. Your supervising attorney has asked you to get her copies of some of the cases cited in opposing counsel's brief. Where can you get copies of those cases for free?
3. You are doing your research on WestlawNext and have found a case that is on point. How can you use the West Key Number System to find other cases that discuss the same point?
4. When might you use A.L.R.?
5. When might you look for a law review article?

8

Researching Constitutional Issues

Constitutional issues can be some of the most interesting, and most time-consuming, issues to research and analyze. Why? Because when you research constitutional issues, you are researching not just the law but also our country's historical underpinnings and ever-changing values.

Like the prior chapters, this chapter has several components: (1) the text, which sets out basic information; (2) exercises, which ask you to apply what you have just read; (3) a quiz that tests the materials set out in the chapter; and (4) an electronic supplement, which shows you how to research a constitutional issue using free sources, Lexis Advance®, WestlawNext™, Bloomberg Law, Lexis.com®, and Westlaw® Classic. To access the supplement, go to *http://www.aspenlawschool.com/books/oates_legalwritinghandbook/*. Your access code to the website is on the card that came with the book. In the ebook, instructions for getting an access code are on the page immediately following the cover page.

§ 8.1   Research Plan for Constitutional Issues

The research plan for constitutional issues is, at its core, the same as the generic research plan set out in Chapter 1: background reading in a secondary source, followed by a search for primary sources; cite checking the primary sources; and, finally, when appropriate, reading additional primary and secondary authorities.

Research Plan for Constitutional Issues

Jurisdiction:	Federal or State
Type of Law:	Constitutional
Issue:	[Set out your issue here.]
Step 1:	If you are unfamiliar with the area of law, spend 30 to 120 minutes doing background reading in a secondary source.
Step 2:	Locate, read, and analyze the applicable constitutional provisions and the cases interpreting and applying those provisions.
Step 3:	Cite check the cases to make sure that they are still good law.
Step 4:	If appropriate, locate and read primary and secondary authorities.

§ 8.2   Sources for Researching Constitutional Issues

§ 8.2.1   Background Reading

Where to start? While the answer to this question is relatively straight-forward for most types of research, when you are talking about constitutional issues, there is not an easy answer. For some issues one source might work well; for other issues looking at that source would be a waste of time.

To figure out what source might work best, ask yourself the following questions.

Question 1:   Does My Issue Involve Federal Constitutional Law, State Constitutional Law, or Both?

If the issue involves federal constitutional law, your best source for background reading will probably be a hornbook or a law review article. If, however, the issue is governed by state constitutional law, a state practice manual or a law review article published in one of your state's law reviews may be the better choice. If your issue involves both federal and state constitutional law, you may need to look in a hornbook, a state practice manual, and law reviews.

Question 2:   Does My Issue Involve an Established or an Emerging Area of Law?

The second question is whether the issue involves an established area of law — for example, a doctrine that you studied in your Constitutional Law class—or a "cutting-edge" or emerging issue. If the issue involves an established area of law, the best source for background reading will probably be a hornbook. For example, see the fifth edition of the *Treatise on Constitutional Law: Substance and Procedure* by Ronald D. Rotunda and John E. Nowak; *American Constitutional Law* by Laurence H. Tribe; or the second edition of *Modern Constitutional Law* by James Antieau. To find these books in your law school library, use your library's online card catalog.

> **PRACTICE POINTER** Some issues involve new twists in established areas. When you are asked to research one of these issues, start by reading about the established area of law in a hornbook, and then look for law review articles about your specific issue. The hornbooks will give you the conceptual framework, and the law review articles will discuss the new twist.

Question 3: Have I Been Asked to Determine Whether a Particular Federal or State Statute Is Constitutional?

If your task includes determining whether a particular federal or state statute is constitutional, you have three options: (1) start by reading about the tests the courts use to determine whether a statute is constitutional; (2) start by reading about the statute; or (3) skip the background reading and begin by cite checking the statute, looking for cases that have discussed whether the statute is constitutional.

Option 1

If you decide to start your research by reading about the tests the courts use in determining whether a statute is constitutional, your best source is a hornbook. Using the hornbook's index, look up the doctrines. For example, look up the words "overbreadth" and "vagueness."

Option 2

If the statute you have been asked to research is a federal statute, the best place to read about the statute is probably the Internet. (See Chapter 5, which describes how to research federal statutes.) Go on Bing, Google, or another search engine, and type in both the full name of the act and, if it has one, its acronym.

Option 3

If the statute has been in effect for more than a few years, think about starting with the statute. In particular, use *Shepard's*®, KeyCite®, or BCite to determine whether any existing cases have discussed the constitutionality of the statute. If there are cases, locate and read the cases.

Exercise 8A	**Background Reading**

If you were assigned to research the following issues, where would you start your research? By doing background reading in a hornbook? By looking for a law review article? By looking for cases that have discussed the statute? Explain your answer.

1. You have been asked to determine whether the local police violated your client's rights when officers searched, without a warrant, a garbage can that he placed on the curb in front of his house.
2. You have been asked to determine whether your client, a high school basketball coach, is a private or a public figure as those terms have been defined by the United States Supreme Court.
3. You have been asked to determine whether a section of the USA PATRIOT Act is constitutional.

§ 8.2.2   Primary Authority

For issues governed by the United States Constitution, your primary authorities will be the United States Constitution itself and the cases that have interpreted and applied it. For issues governed by a state constitution, your primary authorities will be the state constitution itself and state cases interpreting the state constitution.

a.   United States Constitution

The easiest place to find a copy of the United States Constitution is the Internet. For instance, go to Bing, Google, or another search engine, and type in the phrase "United States Constitution." This search will take you to a number of reliable websites, including *http://www.archives.gov/exhibits/charters/constitution_transcript.html*. You can also find the text of the United States Constitution in the first volume of the *United States Code*, the *United States Code Annotated*, the *United States Code Service*, and in most state codes.

b.   Federal Cases Interpreting and Applying the United States Constitution

In looking for cases that have interpreted or applied the United States Constitution, look first for United States Supreme Court decisions; second, for published United States Courts of Appeals decisions from your circuit; third, for published United States Courts of Appeals decisions from other circuits; and finally, for published United States District Court decisions. The following list sets out the abbreviations for the reporters in which each court's decisions can be found.

United States Supreme Court: U.S. (official reporter)
S. Ct. (unofficial reporter)
L. Ed. (unofficial reporter) (1790–1955)
L. Ed. 2d (unofficial) (1956–present)

United States Courts of Appeals: F. (1880–1924)
                                  F.2d (1924–1993)
                                  F.3d (1993–present)
United States District Court: F. Supp. (1933–1998)
                                  F. Supp. 2d (1998–present)

Reporters are available in both book and electronic formats. To find the cases in book form, find where the reporter is located in your library, and then, using the citation, look up the case in the appropriate volume. Similarly, you can use the citation to find copies of the cases on fee-based services such as Lexis Advance, WestlawNext, and Bloomberg Law. Each of these services has the full text of United States Supreme Court decisions, United States Courts of Appeals decisions, and United States District Court decisions.

Increasingly, federal cases are available on free websites, including Google® Scholar and sites maintained by the courts. The following is a list of some of the reliable free websites:

- Google Scholar
- The United States Supreme Court website (*http://www.supremecourtus
  .gov/opinions/opinions.html*)
- Cornell University Legal Information Institute website (*http://www
  .law.cornell.edu/supct*)
- Justia.com
- FindLaw®

c. State Constitutions

Most state constitutions are available on a number of websites. Two of the easiest ways to find copies of a state's constitution are to go on to Bing or Google and search for websites that contain the name of the state and the word "constitution." For example, search for the phrase "Colorado constitution." In addition, you can find links to state constitutions on the Cornell Legal Information Institute site (*http://www.law.cornell.edu/states/listing.html*) and on FindLaw.

d. Cases Interpreting and Applying a State Constitution

The cases interpreting and applying a particular state's constitution can be found in that state's reporters. Look first for decisions from the state's highest appellate court and then for decisions from the state's intermediate court of appeals. To find the names of the reporters in which a particular state's decisions are reported, see Appendix 1 in the *ALWD Citation Manual* and Table 1 in *The Bluebook*.

| **Exercise 8B** | **Primary Authority** |

You have been asked to determine whether a website that sets out "wanted posters" containing the names and addresses of doctors who perform abortions is speech that is protected by the First Amendment or is a "true threat," which is not protected by the First Amendment.

1. Locate a copy of the First Amendment using two of the following sources. Create a screenshot of each of your selected sources that shows the text of the First Amendment.
   a. *http://www.archives.gov/exhibits/charters/constitution.html*
   b. *http://www.house.gov/house/Educate.shtml*
   c. *http://www.law.cornell.edu/constitution/constitution.overview.html*
   d. *http://supreme.justia.com/constitution/*
2. Using each of the following sources, locate a United States Supreme Court case that discusses "true threats."
   a. Lexis.com or Lexis Advance
   b. Westlaw Classic or WestlawNext
   c. Google Scholar
   Describe the process you used to find a case and include a screenshot showing the case you located.
3. Select one of the following states and then locate a website that sets out that state's constitution. Include a screenshot showing the first page of the state's constitution. In addition, indicate whether the online source is searchable and whether it contains citations to cases that have interpreted or applied a particular constitutional provision.
   a. Colorado
   b. New Mexico
   c. Mississippi
   d. The state in which your law school is located

§ 8.2.3   Finding Tools

There are a number of ways to find cases that have interpreted and applied a particular constitutional provision.

- You can find cases by using the citations found in a hornbook, practice manual, or law review article.
- You can find cases by using the Notes of Decisions/Case Notes in an annotated version of a constitution or, if the question is whether a statute is constitutional, in an annotated version of a code.
- You can find cases by using a digest.
- You can find cases by using a fee-based service such as Lexis.com, Lexis Advance, Westlaw Classic, or WestlawNext.
- You can find cases by using *American Law Reports* (A.L.R.).

Exercise 8C   **Finding Tools**

Examine each of the following sources, determining whether they contain citations to cases that discuss the "true threats" doctrine.

1. Locate a constitutional law hornbook. Is there a section in the hornbook that discusses the difference between speech that is protected under the First Amendment and true threats, which are not protected under the First Amendment?
   a. What is the name of the hornbook you consulted?
   b. What chapter or section discusses the First Amendment?
   c. Is there a discussion of true threats?

    d. If there is a discussion of true threats, what cases are cited?
2. Using West's Practice Digest Fourth, locate the topic and key number that discusses true threats.
    a. What is the topic and key number?
    b. Are the cases that are listed the same cases that were listed in the hornbook?
3. Using Lexis Advance or WestlawNext, look for a law review article that discusses the difference between speech that is protected by the First Amendment and true threats, which are not protected by the First Amendment. What is the title of a law review article that is on point? (Include a screenshot of the first page of the article.)

§ 8.2.4   Briefs

In recent years, fee-based services such as Lexis Advance and WestlawNext have added the parties' briefs to their databases. As a result, in addition to finding the text of a court's decision, you may also be able to find copies of briefs that the court considered before writing its opinion. You can use these briefs to find out what each party argued, what authorities each party used to support its arguments, and how each party organized its brief.

Exercise 8D	**Briefs**

1. Using Lexis Advance or WestlawNext, locate the petitioner's brief in *N.A.A.C.P. v. Claiborne Hardware Co.*, 458 U.S. 886 (1982). Include a screenshot showing the first page of the brief.
2. Using Lexis.com, Lexis Advance, Westlaw Classic, or WestlawNext, find the Brief of Plaintiffs-Appellees (Jan. 4, 2000) in *Planned Parenthood v. American Coalition of Life Activists*, 290 F.3d 1058 (9th Cir. 2002).

---

§ 8.3   Using the Research Plan to Research a Constitutional Issue

Just as there are a number of ways to research issues governed by common law, there are also a number of ways to research constitutional issues. Because no one tool is always the best tool, we recommend that you learn to use a number of different tools: free websites and one or more fee-based services.

To learn more about using free and fee-based services to research constitutional issues, see the electronic supplement.

§ 8.3.1   The Assignment
§ 8.3.2   Researching Constitutional Issues Using Free Websites
§ 8.3.3   Researching Constitutional Issues Using Lexis Advance
§ 8.3.4   Researching Constitutional Issues Using WestlawNext
§ 8.3.5   Researching Constitutional Issues Using Bloomberg Law
§ 8.3.6   Researching Constitutional Issues Using Lexis.com
§ 8.3.7   Researching Constitutional Issues Using Westlaw Classic

Chapter 8 Quiz

Draft answers for each of the following questions. Make your points clearly and concisely, and write sentences that are easy to read and that are grammatical and correctly punctuated.

1. Your supervising attorney wants to know whether a court has ruled on the constitutionality of a federal statute. Where should you start your research?
2. If you are arguing a case before the Ninth Circuit Court of Appeals, what would be mandatory authority?
3. How might you use parties' briefs?

Rules

Researching Issues Governed by Federal, State, or Local Court Rules

Congratulations! It is your first day at a summer clerkship at the law firm of your dreams.

Before you have settled in at your desk, one of the partners stops by and tells you that she needs you to find a copy of the Northern District of New York's local rules. She is writing a brief in support of a motion for summary judgment, and she does not know what format the court requires. Thus, she asks you to locate a copy of the applicable local court rule.

As the first partner is walking away from your desk, another partner approaches and tells you that he needs your help. He is representing a man charged with residential burglary and wants you to research ER 609.

You sigh. Although you know how to research issues governed by federal and state statutes and by common law, you haven't a clue about how to research an issue governed by federal or state court rules.

Like the prior chapters, this chapter has several components: (1) the text, which sets out basic information; (2) exercises, which ask you to apply what you have just read; (3) a quiz that tests the materials set out in the chapter; and (4) an electronic supplement, which shows you how to research an issue governed by court rules using free sources, Lexis Advance®, WestlawNext™, Bloomberg Law, Lexis.com®, and Westlaw® Classic. To access the supplement, go to *http://www.aspenlawschool.com/books/oates_legalwritinghandbook/*. Your access code to the website is on the card that came with the book. In the ebook, instructions for getting an access code are on the page immediately following the cover page.

§ 9.1   Research Plans for Projects Involving Federal, State, or Local Court Rules

Most rules questions fall into one of two categories: simple or difficult. The simple questions are usually how, what, and where questions. How many days do I have to file my notice? What should be included in that notice? Where do I file that notice? In contrast, the difficult questions are the questions involving a party's rights. Was the defendant denied his right to a speedy trial? Is a piece of evidence more probative than prejudicial? Is a party entitled to judgment as a matter of law?

When the question falls into the first category, the research is simple. All you need to find is the applicable rule. When, however, the question is a more difficult one, you will need to find not only the rule but the cases that have interpreted and applied that rule. The research plans for these two categories of questions are set out below.

Research Plan for a Simple Rules Question

Jurisdiction: Federal, state, or local

Type of Law: Enacted or court-made

**Preliminary Issue
Statement:**   [Put your first draft of the issue statement here.]

Step 1:   Locate, read, and apply the applicable federal, state, and local rules.

Research Plan for a Difficult Rules Question

Jurisdiction: Federal, state, or local

Type of Law: Enacted or court-made

**Preliminary Issue
Statement:**   [Put your first draft of the issue statement here.]

Step 1:   If you are unfamiliar with the rule in question, spend ten to sixty minutes familiarizing yourself with the rule by reading about the rule in a secondary source.

Step 2:   Locate, read, and analyze the applicable federal, state, or local rules, any comments accompanying the rules, and the cases that have interpreted and applied the rules.

Step 3:   Cite check any cases that you plan to use to make sure they are still good law.

Step 4:   If appropriate, locate and read additional primary and secondary authorities.

§ 9.2   Sources for Federal Rules

"Enacting" federal rules is not an easy process. Proposals for new rules or amendments to existing rules must be submitted to the Judicial Conference, which refers the proposed rule or amendment to the Standing Committee, which refers the proposed rule or amendment to one of five subcommittees. If the subcommittee that receives the proposal believes that the proposal has merit, it sends the proposed rule or amendment out for comment and holds public hearings. If, after these hearings, the subcommittee recommends adoption of the proposed rule or amendment, it refers the proposal back to the Standing Committee, which, if it approves the proposal, sends the proposed rule or amendment to the United States Supreme Court. If the United States Supreme Court approves the rule or amendment, it sends the rule to Congress, which has seven months to approve or reject it. See 28 U.S.C. §§ 2072-2075. Not surprisingly, it usually takes two or three years to enact a new rule or to amend an existing one.

You can find copies of the rules that are eventually "enacted" in a number of sources, including the *United States Code*, the *United States Code Annotated*, the *United States Code Service*; specialized books; a number of free websites; and fee-based, online services (for example, Lexis Advance, WestlawNext, and Bloomberg Law).

§ 9.2.1   *United States Code, United States Code Annotated,* and *United States Code Service*

Because the federal rules are "enacted" by Congress, they are listed in the *United States Code*. For example, the bankruptcy rules are listed in Title 11 of the *United States Code*; the Federal Rules of Criminal Procedure for the United States District Courts are listed in Title 18; and the Federal Rules of Civil Procedure for the United States District Courts are listed in Title 28. While the *United States Code* has just the text of the rules, the *United States Code Annotated* and the *United States Code Service* have the text of the rules, historical notes, cross-references, and notes of decisions.

> **PRACTICE POINTER** Unlike the other parts of the *United States Code*, the rules do not have section numbers. Instead, they have rule numbers. For instance, in the Federal Rules of Civil Procedure, the rule governing summary judgment is called FRCP 56 and, in the Rules of Evidence, the hearsay rule is Rule 802.

§ 9.2.2   Specialized Books

A number of publishing companies publish paperback books containing all or some of the federal rules. For example, LegalPub.com publishes the *Federal Civil Rules Booklet*, which contains not only the Federal Rules of Civil Procedure but also the Federal Rules of Evidence and selected portions of Title 28 of the *United States Code*. Similarly, the National Institute for Trial Advocacy

(NITA) publishes *Federal Rules of Criminal Procedure* and *Federal Rules of Evidence*. Most of these books are replaced or supplemented each year.

There are also a number of books and treatises that provide the text of the rules, in-depth explanations of those rules, and references to key cases. A partial list is set out below. To see what books and treatises are in your library, check your library's electronic card catalog.

> *Federal Civil Rules Handbook* by Baicker-McKee, Janssen & Corr.
> A one-volume book that provides the text of each rule; the authors' commentary, which includes a description of the rule, the rule's purpose and scope, and the core concepts; and citations to key cases.

> *Moore's Federal Practice* (Third Edition).
> A multi-volume treatise that discusses in detail the Rules of Civil Procedure, the Rules of Criminal Procedure, and the United States Courts of Appeals and Supreme Court rules.

> *Federal Practice and Procedure* by Wright, Miller & Kane.
> A multi-volume treatise that discusses the federal rules in detail.

> *Federal Rules of Evidence Manual* (Ninth Edition) by Stephen Saltzberg, Michael M. Martin & Daniel J. Capra.
> A multi-volume treatise that provides the text of each rule; commentary, which includes definitions, an explanation of the rules, and a discussion of the standard of review; and an annotated list of cases.

PRACTICE POINTER   Because most states have modeled their rules after the federal rules, you can use sources such as *Moore's Federal Practice* and *Federal Practice and Procedure* to research both federal and state rules. Just remember to make sure that your state rule is the same as the federal rule.

---

§ 9.2.3   Free Internet Sites

Two of the better free Internet sites for researching rules are LLRX.com, which is at *http://www.llrx.com*, and Cornell's Legal Information Institute (LII) website, which is at *http://www.law.cornell.edu./rules*.

Another good site is the uscourts.gov site. To find a copy of the rules, click on "Rules and Policies," then on "Federal Rules of Practice and Procedure," and lastly on "Current Rules of Practice and Procedure." See *http://www.uscourts .gov/RulesAndPolicies/rules/current-rules.aspx*. Although the U.S. Courts site does not provide links to cases, it does provide you with the text of the rules, summaries of recent changes to the rules, proposed changes to the rules, and links to the federal courts websites, which set out local rules. For more on finding local rules, see section 9.4.

§ 9.2.4   Fee-Based, Online Services

All the fee-based services that have the *United States Code* also have the federal rules. If you know the rule number, you can find the rule by typing the citation into the search box. If you do not know the rule number, you can find the rule by searching for key words.

| **Exercise 9A** | **Federal Rules** |

1. Locate the text of Fed. R. Civ. P. 56 on one of the following websites:
   a. *http://www.law.cornell.edu/rules/frcp/*
   b. *http://www.uscourts.gov/uscourts/rules/civil-procedure.pdf.*
   Create a screenshot of the first page that discusses Fed. R. Civ. P. 56.
2. Find a copy of Fed. R. Civ. P. 56 on both Lexis Advance and WestlawNext and examine the material that follows the text of the rule. What material follows the text of the rule on Lexis Advance? What material follows the text of the rule on WestlawNext? Why is there a difference?

---

§ 9.3   Sources for State Rules

Like the federal rules, state rules are published in a variety of sources.

§ 9.3.1   State Codes

In many states, the state's rules are published in a separate volume of the state's code or integrated into the state's code. If a state has both an unannotated code and an annotated code, the unannotated code will have just the text of the rules, while the annotated code will have the text of the rules, historical notes and cross-references, and Notes of Decisions or Case Notes.

§ 9.3.2   Specialized Books

In most states, either the state or a private publishing company publishes a book setting out all or most of the state's rules. In some instances, these books have just the text of the rules. In other instances, the books have not only the text of the rules but also notes that describe cases that have interpreted or applied the rules. For a list of books for your state, check your law library's electronic catalog or ask a reference librarian.

§ 9.3.3   Free Internet Sites

In most states, you can find a copy of the state's rules using the state courts' home page. Alternatively, go to Bing or Google and type in the name of the state and the word "rules."

§ 9.3.4   Fee-Based, Online Services

If a state's rules are part of its state code, you can find copies of the rules on fee-based, online services, such as Lexis Advance, WestlawNext, or Bloomberg Law. If the state's rules are not part of the state code, you may or may not be able to find copies of the rules on the fee-based services. To find out if the rules are on your service, either do a database search or call your representative or the service's help number.

Look for your state's summary judgment rule in each of the following sources. In most states, this will be Civil Rule 56.

a   Your state's website or another free website. Create a screenshot showing the URL and the rule.

b.   Either Lexis Advance or WestlawNext. Create a screenshot showing the rule.

§ 9.4   Sources for Local Rules

Most of the federal and state rules allow the courts within their jurisdiction to adopt their own local rules. Generally, these rules establish the procedures and timelines for filing various papers with the court and the formats that the judges want parties to use. In addition, in many jurisdictions, the local rules include sample forms.

> **PRACTICE POINTER**   No matter what source you use, always make sure that the local rules you have located are the rules that are currently in effect.

§ 9.4.1   Books

Sometimes you can find a copy of a court's local rules in a book. For instance, *Federal Local Courts Rules* is a multivolume set published by West, a Thomson Reuters business, that provides the local rules for the United States federal courts. Some circuits also have their own books. For example, in *Federal Ninth Circuit Civil Appellate Practice*, author Christopher A. Goelz walks you through the process of filing and arguing an appeal in the Ninth Circuit Court of Appeals.

§ 9.4.2   Free Internet Sites

The easiest place to find a copy of a court's local rules is on a free Internet site. You can, for instance, find the local rules for federal courts using the links on the United States Courts' website: Go to *http://www.uscourts.gov/ Court_Locator/CourtWebsites.aspx* and select the appropriate court. Alternatively, use the links on *http://www.llrx.com/courtrules.*

Similarly, to find the local rules for a state court, select a search engine and, using the advanced search option, insert the name of the court and the word "rules."

§ 9.4.3   Fee-Based, Online Services

You can also find local rules on fee-based, online services, such as Lexis Advance, WestlawNext, and Bloomberg Law.

§ 9.4.4   Telephone Calls and Emails

If you cannot find a copy of the local rules in a book, on a free Internet site, or on a fee-based service, call or email the court clerk.

PRACTICE POINTER	As a practicing attorney, keep abreast of proposed changes to the rules by regularly reading your local bar bulletin or checking the local bar's web page and the court's web page.

Exercise 9C   Local Rules

Locate the United States District Court for the Northern District of California's local rules governing the notice requirements for motions for summary judgment using one of the following sources:

a. A free website. For example, can you find a copy of the local rule using the links on http://www .uscourts.gov/Court_Locator/CourtWebsites.aspx? Create a screenshot showing the applicable rule.
b. A fee-based service (Lexis Advance or WestlawNext). Create a screenshot showing the applicable rule.

§ 9.5   Using the Research Plan to Research an Issue Governed by Federal, State, or Local Court Rules

In researching issues governed by federal, state, or local rules, you have a number of options: You can research the issue using books and fee-based services like WestlawNext, Lexis Advance, or Bloomberg Law. However, in almost all instances, the best option is a free website.

To learn more about using free and fee-based services to research issues governed by court rules, see the electronic supplement, especially section 9.5.2.

§ 9.5.1   The Assignment
§ 9.5.2   Researching an Issue Governed by Federal, State, or Local Court Rules Using Free Websites
§ 9.5.3   Researching an Issue Governed by Federal, State, or Local Court Rules Using Lexis Advance
§ 9.5.4   Researching an Issue Governed by Federal, State, or Local Court Rules Using WestlawNext

Chapter 9 Quiz

Draft answers for each of the following questions. Make your points clearly and concisely, and write sentences that are easy to read and that are grammatical and correctly punctuated.

1. Where can you find a copy of the Federal Rules of Civil Procedure and Notes of Decisions/Case Notes for cases that have discussed those rules?
2. Where can you find an in-depth discussion of the Federal Rules of Civil Procedure?
3. Where is the easiest place to find copies of the local rules for the United States Courts of Appeals?

Cite Checking

Citators

ne of the most embarrassing things that can happen to you as an attorney is to discover that the case you are relying on was either reversed on appeal or overruled in a subsequent case. The conversation usually goes something like this:

Attorney: Your Honor, our case is almost identical to *State v. Smith*, a 2013 Court of Appeals decision. In that case, . . .
Judge (interrupting the attorney): Counsel, are you aware that that decision was reversed by the Supreme Court earlier this month?
Attorney: (long pause) No, your Honor. I was not.

To make sure you do not find yourself in this position, cite check every case that you include in your memos and briefs. In addition, cite check every case that your opponent relies on in its brief. One of the easiest ways to win a case is to show that the authority on which the other side has relied is no longer good law.

Like the earlier chapters, this chapter has several components: (1) the text, which sets out basic information; (2) exercises, which ask you to apply what you have just read; (3) a quiz that tests the materials set out in the chapter; and (4) an electronic supplement, which shows you how to cite check using *Shepard's®*, KeyCite®, and BCite, which is on Bloomberg Law. To access the supplement, go to *http://www.aspenlawschool.com/books/oates_legalwriting handbook/*. Your access code to the website is on the card that came with the book. In the ebook, instructions for getting an access code are on the page immediately following the cover page.

§ 10.1   Introduction to Citators

Citators serve two purposes. First, they are used to determine whether a particular authority, for example, a case, is still good law. Second, they are used to find other authorities that have cited to a particular case, statute, regulation, law review article, or other authority.

Case citators work as follows. Each time a court publishes a decision, an attorney who works for the company that produces the citator reads the case and determines whether the case reverses or overrules an earlier decision. A decision is reversed when, in the same case, a higher court reverses the decision of a lower court. In contrast, a case is overruled when, in a different case, a court determines that, in an earlier decision, the court applied the wrong rule of law.

After determining whether the case reverses or overrules an earlier decision, the attorney who works for the company that publishes the citator examines each of the cases that are cited in the new case, determining how, in that new case, the court treats the cases that it cites. Does the court apply the rule or rules set out in the case, distinguish the case, criticize the court's reasoning, or do something else (for example, simply cite the case)? This information is then collected and placed in the citator. For example, if in Case D, the court distinguishes Case A, that fact will be indicated in the citator under Case A. Similarly, if Case D follows Case B, that fact will be indicated in the citator under Case B.

In addition to cite checking cases, you can also cite check a variety of other sources. For example, if you want to find cases that have cited to a particular statute, you can cite check that statute. Similarly, if you want to find cases that have cited to a particular restatement section or to a particular law review article, you can cite check those sources.

§ 10.2   Types of Citators

Although historically attorneys checked their citations using the book version of one of *Shepard's* Citators, today most attorneys do their cite checking online using the online version of *Shepard's*, which is on Lexis.com® and Lexis Advance®; or KeyCite®, which is on Westlaw® Classic and WestlawNext™; or BCite, which is on Bloomberg Law. The online versions of *Shepard's*, KeyCite, and BCite provide the attorney with more up-to-date information than the book version of *Shepard's* and are easier to use.

> **PRACTICE POINTER**   Just as individuals who ask you to Xerox a case are not asking you to copy a case using a machine sold by Xerox, attorneys who ask you to *Shepardize* a case are not asking you to cite check the case using *Shepard's*. They are simply asking you to check the case to make sure that it is still good law, and you can do that using *Shepard's*, KeyCite, or BCite.

Because determining whether a source is still good law must be done source by source by someone trained in the law, to date there are no free sources that provide all of the information contained in *Shepard's*, KeyCite, or BCite. While the "How cited" option that is on Google® Scholar lists citing cases, it does not provide you with the subsequent history or tell you how later cases treated the case that you are cite checking.

§ 10.3   Cite Checking Using *Shepard's*, KeyCite, and BCite

To learn more about using free and fee-based services to cite check, see the electronic supplement.

§ 10.3.1 Cite Checking Using *Shepard's*
§ 10.3.2 Cite Checking Using KeyCite
§ 10.3.3 Cite Checking Using BCite
§ 10.3.4 Cite Checking Using Free Websites

Exercise 10A   *Shepard's*

1. Is *Harbert v. Healthcare Services Group, Inc.*, 391 F.3d 1140 (10th Cir. 2004), still good law?
2. What is the name of a Third Circuit Court of Appeals decision that cited *Harbert* for the point of law set out in headnote 8 in *Harbert*?

Exercise 10B   KeyCite

1. Is *Harbert v. Healthcare Services Group, Inc.*, 391 F.3d 1140 (10th Cir. 2004), still good law?
2. Is the point of law set out in headnote 8 in the Lexis Advance version of the case the same as the point of the law set out in headnote 8 in the WestlawNext version of the case?
3. Did the United States Supreme Court accept review?

Exercise 10C   BCite

1. Is *Harbert v. Healthcare Services Group, Inc.*, 391 F.3d 1140 (10th Cir. 2004), still good law?
2. Is the point of law set out in headnote 8 in the Bloomberg Law version of the case the same as the point of law set out in headnote 8 in either the Lexis Advance version of the case or in headnote 8 in the WestlawNext version of the case?
3. Can you determine which cases have cited Harbert for a particular headnote?

Chapter 10 Quiz

Draft answers for each of the following questions. Make your points clearly and concisely, and write sentences that are easy to read and that are grammatical and correctly punctuated.

1. If an attorney asks you to *Shepardize* a case, what is the attorney asking you to do?
2. What are the two ways in which citators can be used?
3. What does it mean when someone says that a court's decision was reversed? That a court's decision was overruled?

Legislative Histories

Doing Federal and State Legislative Histories

T here was a time when, if a judge or partner asked you to do a legislative history, you knew that you were being tested or punished.
Back then, doing a legislative history meant spending days in the
basement of a large law library, working your way through stacks
of dusty federal documents. The good news is that legislative
histories are much easier to do today. The key is knowing what to look for and
where to look for it.

Like the prior chapters, this chapter has a number of components: the text,
exercises, and a quiz. In addition, the supplement walks you through doing a
legislative history using both free and online services. To access the supplement, go to *http://www.aspenlawschool.com/books/oates_legalwritinghandbook*.
Your access code to the website is on the card that came with the book. In the
ebook, instructions for getting an access code are on the page immediately
following the cover page.

§ 11.1 What Is a Legislative History, and Why Would You Do One?

A legislative history is the history of a piece of legislation. You can do
legislative history for federal statutes and, in most states, for at least some
state statutes.

Attorneys and judges do legislative histories to determine why a statute
was enacted and how the body that enacted the statute wanted the statute

interpreted.[1] Consequently, if you are working as a law clerk for a judge, the judge may ask you to do a legislative history to help him or her decide how to interpret a particular statute. Similarly, if you are working for an attorney, the attorney may ask you to do a legislative history to determine whether he or she can use that history to support a client's argument.

Although there are some judges who find legislative histories persuasive, in recent years the courts have relied on them less and less.[2] Some judges reject legislative histories because, like Justice Antonin Scalia, they believe that the only legitimate interpretive guide is the text of the statute. Other judges reject legislative histories because they do not believe that they can determine what the legislative body as a whole intended. Because doing a legislative history can be time consuming, do not do one unless you are specifically asked to do so, or unless you determine that the judge to whom you are writing will find a legislative history persuasive.

§ 11.2   When You Do a Legislative History, What Are You Looking For?

When you do a legislative history, you are looking for the documents that were created as part of the process of enacting or amending a piece of legislation. Table 11.1 summarizes the steps that a bill goes through when it is introduced into the United States House of Representatives and the documents that would be produced at each step. The steps and the documents would be the same for a bill that is introduced in the United States Senate. At the state level, the steps would be similar but not as many documents would be produced, and the names of the documents might be different.

For more detailed information on the legislative process, see *How Our Laws Are Made* by Charles W. Johnson, Parliamentarian, United States House of Representatives, which is available at *http://thomas.loc.gov/home/lawsmade .toc.html*, or *Enactment of a Law* by Robert B. Dove, Parliamentarian, United States Senate, which is available at *http://thomas.loc.gov/home/enactment/ enactlawtoc.html*.

> **PRACTICE POINTER** While a complete legislative history would include all documents produced during the legislative process, you will not always need all these documents. For instance, sometimes you can make your argument from just the committee reports.

---

1. *See, e.g.,* Stephen Breyer, *On the Uses of Legislative History in Interpreting Statutes*, 65 S. Cal. L. Rev. 845 (1992).

2. *See* Michael H. Koby, *The Supreme Court's Declining Reliance on Legislative History: The Impact of Justice Scalia's Critique*, 36 Harv. J. on Legis. 369 (1999).

Table 11.1	How a House Bill Becomes Law	
STEP		**DOCUMENTS**
1. A member of the House of Representatives introduces the bill.		Bill Congressional Record
2. The bill is referred to a committee. The committee may then refer the bill to a subcommittee. (Most bills die in committee.)		Hearings Committee Print
3. If the bill does not die in committee, the committee submits its report on the bill to the House.		Committee Report
4. The bill is presented to the House for debate, amendments, and a vote.		Congressional Record Engrossed Bill
5. If the bill is approved, it is sent to the Senate. The Senate repeats steps 1-4.		Congressional Record Engrossed Bill
6. If the Senate passes the bill, it returns the bill, with any amendments, to the House. The House then approves the amendments, determines that the amendments are unacceptable, or creates a Conference Committee to create a compromise bill.		Congressional Record Conference Committee Report Enrolled Bill
7. If both the House and the Senate pass the same version of the bill, the bill is sent to the President for signature. If the President signs the bill, it becomes law.		Presidential Statement Public Law

§ 11.3   Research Plan for Doing a Legislative History

While on the surface the research plan for doing a legislative history looks very different from the research plan for doing statutory research, when you look deeper, you find that the steps are essentially the same: (1) Looking for a summary is similar to doing background reading, (2) looking for a compiled legislative history or doing your own legislative history is the same as locating primary authority, and (3) looking for amendments is the same as cite checking. Thus, while the surface features are different, the underlying structure is the same.

Research Plan for Legislative Histories

Jurisdiction: Federal or State

Type of Law: Enacted law

Preliminary Issue
Statement: [Put your first draft of the issue statement here.]

Step 1:   Look for cases or law review articles that have summarized the statute's legislative history. If the cases or law review articles give you the information that you need, stop researching. If, however, you cannot find a summary or you want to look at the documents cited in the cases or law review articles, go to Step 2.

Step 2:   Look for a compiled legislative history.

Step 3:   If you cannot find a compiled legislative history, assemble your own legislative history.

Step 4:   If appropriate, look for recent amendments that did not pass.

§ 11.4   Sources for Legislative Histories

Because legislative histories take so long to compile, when you are asked to do a history, look first to see whether someone else has already compiled one.

§ 11.4.1   Summaries

If all you need is a summary of a statute's legislative history, look for a case or a law review article that summarizes the statute's legislative history. If you find a summary, you can use the citations from the summary to locate the key documents. For example, if the case or article refers to a committee report, use the citation to the report to locate the report using free websites.

> **PRACTICE POINTER**   Although you can do a separate search for summaries of legislative histories, most often you will run across them in the course of your research. Therefore, it is often best to postpone doing a legislative history until you have done the rest of your research.

§ 11.4.2   Compiled Legislative Histories

A compiled legislative history is a book, notebook, file folder, or website that sets out some or all of the documents created during the process of enacting a particular piece of legislation. Unlike summaries, which simply summarize the legislative history, these compiled histories include copies of the documents. For example, a compiled legislative history may have the marked-up copy of the bill, transcripts of hearings, copies of committee reports, excerpts from the floor debate, and the President's or governor's statement.

Here are some of the best sources for compiled legislative histories:

- LLSDC's Legislative Source Book, which is available at *http://www .llsdc.org/sourcebook/.*
- *United States Code Congressional and Administrative News* (U.S.C.C.A.N.), which is available in book form and on Lexis Advance® and WestlawNext™.

- Nancy Johnson, *Sources of Compiled Legislative Histories* (2000), which is available in book form and on HeinOnline (*http://home.heinonline .org*)
- Lexis.com®, Westlaw® Classic, and WestlawNext legislative histories databases

Exercise 11A   Locating Compiled Legislative History

Using WestlawNext, locate a compiled legislative history for the Family and Medical Leave Act.

- Sign onto WestlawNext, select the "Content" tab, and then click on "Statutes and Court Rules."
- Look through the list that is on the right-hand side of the page and select "Legislative History."
- Select "Arnold & Porter Legislative Histories" and scroll through your search results, looking to see whether there is an entry related to the Family and Medical Leave Act. When you find the entry, click on that entry and then identify the link that sets out the table of contents.

a. Who is it that assembled the legislative history?
b. What types of documents are set in the compiled legislative history?

§ 11.4.3   Sources for Assembling Your Own Legislative History

If you cannot find a compiled legislative history, you will need to compile your own. For instructions on how to compile a legislative history for a federal statute, see Richard J. McKinney & Ellen A. Sweet, Federal Legislative History Research: A Practitioner's Guide to Compiling the Documents and Sifting for Legislative Intent, at *http://www.llsdc.org/fed-leg-hist*.

§ 11.5   A Note About State Legislative Histories

Although historically it was difficult, if not impossible, to do a legislative history for a state statute, that is changing. Using the Internet and government files, you can now find the legislative history for at least some state statutes.

If you need to do a legislative history for a state statute, start by going onto Bing or Google and search for websites that describe how to do a legislative history in your state.

Exercise 11B   State Legislative Histories

Using Bing or Google, determine whether there is a website that tells you how to do a legislative history for California statutes. If there is a website, record the URL for that website.

§11.6 Using the Research Plan to Do a Legislative History

In doing a federal or state legislative history, you have a number of options: You can research the history using books, fee-based services such as Lexis Advance and WestlawNext, or free websites. In this section, we walk you through the process of doing a legislative history in five different ways. While you do not need to go through each subsection, do go through several, comparing and contrasting the advantages and disadvantages of each.

§ 11.6.1   The Assignment
§ 11.6.2   Doing a Legislative History Using Free Websites
§ 11.6.3   Doing a Legislative History Using Lexis Advance
§ 11.6.4   Doing a Legislative History Using WestlawNext
§ 11.6.5   Doing a Legislative History Using Bloomberg Law
§ 11.6.6   Doing a Legislative History Using Lexis.com
§ 11.6.7   Doing a Legislative History Using Westlaw Classic

Chapter 11 Quiz

Draft answers for each of the following questions. Make your points clearly and concisely, and write sentences that are easy to read and that are grammatical and correctly punctuated.

1. What is a legislative history?
2. Where can you find a summary of a statute's or an act's legislative history?
3. What types of documents are typically included in a compiled legislative history?
4. If you are asked to do a legislative history for a state statute, what should you do first?

Practice Information

Locating Forms

A lthough there is far more to practicing law than filling out forms, there will be days when you feel like that is all you do. Sometimes these forms will be specific ones that the courts require—for example, when you are helping a client file for a divorce or for bankruptcy. At other times, you will take forms that others have developed and modify them to meet your client's needs—for example, you may modify a standard form contract, lease, or will.

As you begin reading this chapter, once again note that the chapter has several components: (1) the text, which sets out basic information; (2) exercises, which ask you to apply what you have just read; (3) a quiz that tests the materials set out in the chapter; and (4) an electronic supplement, which shows you how to locate forms using free sources, Lexis Advance®, WestlawNext™, Bloomberg Law, Lexis.com®, and Westlaw® Classic. To access the supplement, go to *http://www.aspenlawschool.com/books/oates_legalwritinghandbook/*. Your access code to the website is on the card that came with the book. In the ebook, instructions for getting an access code are on the page immediately following the cover page.

§ 12.1 Forms on Court Websites

If a court requires specific forms, those forms are probably on the court's website. To find them, simply go to Bing or Google or a similar search engine, and search for the name of the court and the word "forms."

The attorney for whom you work has asked you to find a copy of the form used in Washington to request a modification of child custody. Locate the Washington courts' website, find a copy of the form, and make a screenshot of the first page of the form.

§ 12.2   Forms on Government and Other Websites

You can also find copies of forms on a number of other websites. While some will provide the forms for free; others charge a fee.

One of the best sources for federal forms is SearchUSA.gov, which allows you to search either by keyword or by agency. Another useful site is Justia.com, which provides links not only to federal forms but also to thousands of state and business forms.

Unless the form is one prescribed by the courts, do not use a sample form without first reviewing the law to make sure the form satisfies the law in the applicable jurisdiction. In addition, make sure that you modify the form so it meets your client's needs and goals.

§ 12.3   Forms on Fee-Based Sites

Historically, attorneys found sample forms in "form books," that is, books containing sample forms. Although you can still find those books in most law libraries, many of them are now available online through fee-based services such as Lexis Advance, WestlawNext, and Bloomberg Law.

One way to find forms on Lexis Advance is to select the appropriate pre-search filters. For example, if you need to draft a lease for property located in California, select "Forms," California," and "Real Property." (See section 12.5.3 in the electronic supplement for more information.) On WestlawNext, select "Forms," "California," and then "Real Estate." (See section 12.5.4 in the electronic supplement for more information.) While Bloomberg Law does not have copies of leases, it does have other types of forms. To see them, click on the "Transactional Law" tab.

You have been asked to draft a contract to buy and sell commercial real estate located in Colorado. Using Lexis Advance and WestlawNext, locate a sample document and make a screenshot of the first page.

§ 12.4 Practice Manuals and CLE Materials

State practice manuals and Continuing Legal Education (CLE) materials are also good sources for sample forms. CLE programs are short courses (one to seven hours) designed for practicing attorneys. These programs are often taught by the best attorneys in the state, and as part of their presentations, these attorneys prepare written materials that provide information about the topic and, if applicable, sample forms.

You can usually find state practice manuals and CLE materials in your local law library. In addition, some practice manuals are available on fee-based services. For example, the practice manuals published by West are available on Westlaw Classic and WestlawNext.

§ 12.5 Locating Forms

As with other types of research, when it comes time to look for forms, you have a number of options. Because no one option stands out as the best option, take the time to see what is available both on free websites and on one or more fee-based services.

To learn more about using free and fee-based services to locate forms, see the electronic supplement.

Chapter 12 Quiz

Draft answers for each of the following questions. Make your points clearly and concisely, and write sentences that are easy to read and that are grammatical and correctly punctuated.

1. Where would be a good place to find government forms, for example, Social Security forms?
2. Where would be a good place to find a Uniform Commercial Code Financing Form (UCC1)?
3. What are continuing legal education (CLE) materials?

Researching Judges, Law Firms, People, Companies, and Things

Like cigarettes, this chapter comes with a warning. While the tools described in this chapter can make your life as a law student and lawyer much easier, they can also make it much more difficult. What you can find out about other people, other people can find out about you and the people and companies you represent.

Like the prior chapters, this chapter has several components: (1) the text, which sets out basic information; (2) exercises, which ask you to apply what you have just read; (3) a quiz that tests the materials set out in the chapter; and (4) an electronic supplement, which shows you how to research judges, law firms, people, companies, and things using free sources, Lexis Advance®, WestlawNext™, Bloomberg Law, Lexis.com®, and Westlaw® Classic. To access the supplement, go to *http://www.aspenlawschool.com/books/oates_legalwrit inghandbook/*. Your access code to the website is on the card that came with the book. In the ebook, instructions for getting an access code are on the page immediately following the cover page.

§ 13.1 Researching Judges

As a law student, you may want to research a judge before applying for an externship or clerkship; as an attorney, you may want to research a judge before writing a brief to that judge or before appearing before that judge.

§ 13.1.1 Court Websites

In some jurisdictions, the cheapest and easiest way to find out some basic information about a judge is to use the court's website. You can find the website using a search engine. For example, go to Bing or Google and then type in the name of the court and the judge's name.

§ 13.1.2 Fee-Based Services

If you cannot find information about the judge on the court's website, your next best bet is a fee-based service such as Lexis Advance, WestlawNext, or Bloomberg Law. You can use these services to find not only biographical information about judges but also the text of opinions that they have authored and, in some jurisdictions, their current dockets. To find biographical information, identify the databases containing biographical information.

Exercise 13A   Researching Judges

You have been invited to interview with Douglas H. Ginsburg, a Senior Judge for the United States Court of Appeals for the District of Columbia. Before you go on the interview, you want to "research" Judge Ginsburg, finding where he went to law school, what he did before becoming a judge, and copies of one or two of the more recent opinions that he authored.

1. Locate the United States Court of Appeals for the District for Columbia's website using Bing or Google or the links on *http://www.uscourts.gov*. Does the court's website tell you where Judge Douglas Howard Ginsburg went to law school? What he has done since he graduated from law school? The names of recent opinions that Judge Ginsburg has authored? Set out the answers that you are able to locate.

2. Can you find the answers to the questions set out above using Lexis Advance, WestlawNext, or Bloomberg Law? Select one of these services and then answer the following questions. Does the service tell you where Judge Ginsburg went to law school? What he has done since he graduated from law school? The names of recent opinions that Judge Ginsburg has authored? Set out the answers that you were able to locate.

3. Using Bing or Google, look for a picture of Judge Ginsburg. Make a screenshot of a website that contains a picture of Judge Ginsburg.

---

§ 13.2   Researching Law Firms and Attorneys

In addition to researching judges, you will often need to research law firms and attorneys, either because you would like to work for the firm or attorney or because the firm or attorney is representing an opposing party. The sources for this type of research are similar to the sources that you used in researching judges.

§ 13.2.1 Websites

The easiest and cheapest way to find about a law firm or an attorney is on the Internet. Simply pick a search engine, and type in the name of the law firm.

§ 13.2.2 Fee-Based Services

You can also find information on fee-based services such as Lexis Advance, WestlawNext, or Bloomberg Law. For example, on WestlawNext, you can find decisions in which a particular attorney was the attorney of record by selecting the cases database and then running the following search: AT(Attorney's name).

Exercise 13B	**Researching Attorneys**

You have been invited to interview with an attorney (your professor will provide you with the name of a local attorney). Before going to the interview, you want to research this attorney, finding where he or she went to law school, the area or areas of law in which he or she practices, and, if possible, the names of some of his or her clients.

1. Does the attorney or the attorney's firm have a website? If the attorney or firm has a website, look for answers to the following questions. Does it tell you where the attorney went to law school? The types of law the attorney practices? The names of some of the attorney's clients? Set out the information that you were able to locate.
2. Is there a reference to the attorney or the attorney's firm on Lexis Advance, WestlawNext, or Bloomberg Law? Select one of these services and then look for answers to the following questions. Does the service tell you where the attorney went to law school? The types of law the attorney practices? The names of some of the attorney's clients? Set out the information that you were able to locate.
3. Can you find a picture of the attorney using Bing or Google or another search engine? If you can, make a screenshot of that picture.

§ 13.3   Locating and Researching People

Of all the types of non-legal research that you will do as an attorney, researching people is probably the most controversial. How deep should you dig when researching your own client, opposing parties, victims, witnesses, and jurors?

§ 13.3.1 Finding Mailing Addresses, Phone Numbers, and Email Addresses

There are now literally hundreds of websites that will provide you with an individual's mailing address, home phone number, and age for free. For practice, try locating your address and phone number using the following sites:

- InfoSpace, which is *at http://www.infospace.com*
- 411.com, which is at *http://www.411.com*

There is, however, almost always a fee for other information, for example, for email addresses, and there are no guarantees as to reliability. As a consequence, you may want to choose to use one of the fee-based services such as Lexis Advance, WestlawNext, or Bloomberg Law.

> **PRACTICE POINTER** Under your law school subscription, you may not be able to access the databases containing information about individuals.

§ 13.3.2 Finding Public Records

Many public records are now on the Internet. Although you can find some of these records on free government or commercial sites, the easiest and fastest way to find public records is through a fee-based service such as Lexis Advance, WestlawNext, or Bloomberg Law. All three of these services contain a variety of public records, including professional license records, real estate records, voting records, and records of prior convictions.

§ 13.4 Researching Companies

While you can usually find more information about publicly held companies than privately held companies, you can almost always find at least something about every company. Start by looking at the company's own website, then at government websites, then at fee-based services, and finally at news articles, if available.

§ 13.4.1 Company Websites

Today most companies have a website. To find that website, select a search engine, for example, Bing or Google, and type in the name of the company and variations on that name.

If the company that you are researching is traded publicly, you can find information about that company on the United States Securities and Exchange Commission website, which is called "EDGAR." See *http://www.sec.gov/edgar/searchedgar/companysearch.html*. This site has most SEC filings: quarterly and annual reports, listings of officers, and prospectuses.

Similar information can be found through the offices of the secretaries of state for the various states. In searching for companies, keep in mind that the name that you see on the sign in front of the company may not be the company's official name.

§ 13.4.2 Fee-Based Services

You can use Lexis Advance, WestlawNext, and Bloomberg Law to find information about companies and the people who work for them. For example, both Lexis Advance and WestlawNext have Hoover's Company Profiles, which has information on thousands of private and public companies, providing not only the company's name, address, and phone and fax numbers but also the names of its officers, a summary of operations, and some financial information. In addition, all three services have a number of other products.

Exercise 13C	**Researching Companies**

Before filing a suit against Gentex Inc., you need to find as much information as you can about the company.

1. What information is on Gentex's website? Make a screenshot of the page designed for investors.
2. What information can you find about Gentex on EDGAR? Locate the information using a free website and create a screenshot of the first page that discusses Gentext.
3. What information can you find about Gentex on Lexis Advance, WestlawNext, or Bloomberg Law? Select one of these services, and create a screenshot of the first page of a document that discusses Gentex.

§ 13.5   Sources to Use in Preparing for Litigation

You can now use the Internet to find much of the information that you will need in preparing for litigation. In addition to using the Internet to locate information about judges and attorneys (see sections 13.1 and 13.2), you can also use it to find experts, jury verdicts in similar cases, similar cases that are pending in the courts, information about medical conditions, products, and almost anything else that might be at issue in any given case. The trick is to find reliable information quickly.

§ 13.5.1   Experts

If you do litigation, you will frequently need to identify the perfect expert witness or research the other side's experts. One of the best ways to find an expert is to search university websites, looking for individuals who have the type of expertise you need. Another way is "word of mouth": Attorneys who have handled similar cases may be able to refer you to an appropriate expert. You may also be able to find an expert using a site such as the legal professional portion of FindLaw. For example, "FindLaw for Legal Professionals" has links to individuals who work as experts.

In addition, a number of special interest organizations list and evaluate experts. For instance, members of the American Association for Justice (AAJ) (formerly the Association of Trial Lawyers of America) can find experts using AAJ's website, which is at *http://www.justice.org*. You can also find lists of experts on Lexis Advance, WestlawNext, and Bloomberg Law.

PRACTICE POINTER	Although there will be times when you need to use a "professional expert," many attorneys believe that individuals who are not associated with a particular group or who do not testify for a living

make more credible and, therefore, more persuasive witnesses.

Exercise 13D   **Researching Experts**

1. You need to find an automobile accident reconstruction expert in Kansas City, Missouri. Using FindLaw for Legal Professionals (*http://lp.findlaw.com/*) and either Lexis Advance or WestlawNext find the name of a possible expert witness. Include a screenshot from lp.findlaw.com that shows the name of the expert and a screenshot from either Lexis Advance or WestlawNext that shows the name of the expert.
2. Google the expert that you located. What type of information can you find about the expert? Include at least one screenshot from a website that has information about the expert.

§ 13.5.2 Jury Verdicts

Lexis Advance and WestlawNext have databases that contain information about jury verdicts. For example, you can use Lexis Advance's and WestlawNext's Jury Verdicts and Settlements' databases to research verdicts in cases involving a particular party, a particular expert, a particular judge, or a particular type of accident or injury.

§ 13.5.3 Dockets and Pending Litigation

In many jurisdictions, you can find a copy of a particular court's docket on the court's website. For example, the federal courts now have their dockets on their court websites. In addition, you can find copies of court dockets and documents on free websites such as Justia.com.

Exercise 13E   **Researching Dockets**

Using *http://dockets.justia.com/*, locate a copy of the docket for the United States District Court for the Northern District of Florida that shows civil rights cases that have been filed.

§ 13.5.4 Jury Instructions

Lexis Advance and WestlawNext also have jury instructions.

§ 13.6   Finding Medical Information

§ 13.6.1 Books

Most large public and law libraries have at least one or two books that describe various medical conditions. Three good sources are *Merck Manual of Medical Information*, published by Pocket; the American Medical Association's *Complete Medical Encyclopedia*, published by Random House; and the *Concise Dictionary of Medical-Legal Terms: A General Guide to Interpretation and Usage*, published by CRC Press-Parthenon Publishers.

§ 13.6.2 Free Websites

There are a number of good free Internet sites. Try, for example, the National Institutes of Health's Medline, which is at *http://www.nlm.nih.gov.* This easy-to-use site is designed for both medical professionals and the public. In the alternative, try NIH's PubMed at *http://www.pubmedcentral.nih.gov,* which provides a free digital archive of biomedical and life sciences journal literature.

§ 13.6.3 Fee-Based Services

Lexis.com and WestlawNext have a number of medical databases. For a list of these databases, see the electronic supplement.

§ 13.7   Finding Information About Products

§ 13.7.1 Books

One of the best sources for information about products is the LDR's *Lawyers Desk Reference* by Philo, Atkinson & Philo, Jr. If you do not have time to read the entire set, read chapter 9 in volume 2. This chapter lists the questions that you should ask about a product and lists a variety of directories that may contain pertinent information.

§ 13.7.2 Free Websites

Both Cornell's Legal Information Institute site (LII) and the legal professional portion of FindLaw.com have information on product liability. To find information on the LII site, go to *http://www.law.cornell.edu*, click on the "Wex legal encyclopedia," and run a search for the phrase "product liability." This site will retrieve a short description of product liability law plus links to useful information.

You can also find product liability information on the U.S. Consumer Product Safety Commission website, which is at *http://www.cpsc.gov.*

A valuable source for cutting-edge technology and theory is *Scientific American* magazine. You can find the current edition in most libraries, and older articles are archived online at *http://www.sciam.com.* The *Scientific American* website is easy to use and has a mix of free and for-purchase articles.

§ 13.7.3 Fee-Based Services

Lexis Advance and WestlawNext have databases related to products liability. For more information about these databases, see the supplement.

§ 13.8   Locating Information

The best tool for locating information about judges, law firms, people, companies, and things depends on the type of information you need. Sometimes a free source is the best option; at other times, a particular fee-based service may be best. Consequently, you need to be familiar with a variety of different tools.

To learn more about using free and fee-based services to locate information, see the electronic supplement.

§ 13.8.1 The Assignment
§ 13.8.2 Locating Forms Using Free Websites
§ 13.8.3 Locating Forms Using Lexis Advance
§ 13.8.4 Locating Forms Using WestlawNext
§ 13.8.5 Locating Forms Using Bloomberg Law
§ 13.8.6 Locating Forms Using Lexis.com
§ 13.8.7 Locating Forms Using Westlaw Classic

Chapter 13 Quiz

Draft answers for each of the following questions. Make your points clearly and concisely, and write sentences that are easy to read and that are grammatical and correctly punctuated.

1. As a practicing attorney, where would you begin your search for information about a particular company?
2. As a practicing attorney, where could you find information about the amounts juries have awarded in cases that are factually similar to your case?
3. What is a reliable website that contains information about various medical conditions?

Glossary of Sources for Legal Research

Advance Sheets Advance sheets are paperback pamphlets that contain copies of recent published decisions. They are usually filed at the end of a set of reporters and are used to keep the book version of the reporter up to date.

ALWD Citation Manual The *ALWD Citation Manual*, which is published by Aspen Law and Business, sets out rules for citing to constitutions, statutes, cases, secondary sources, and other materials in legal memos and briefs.

***American Jurisprudence* (Am. Jur.)** American Jurisprudence (Am. Jur.) is a comprehensive multi-volume legal encyclopedia that is available both in book form and on Lexis.com®, LexisAdvance®, Westlaw® Classic, and WestlawNext™. Am. Jur. has over 440 articles, covering a wide range of legal topics. The topics are set out in alphabetical order and include references to selected cases and to A.L.R. annotations. Am. Jur. is not jurisdiction specific: Instead of setting out federal law or a particular state's law, it discusses the law in general terms. Most attorneys use Am. Jur. as a finding tool to obtain an overview of an area of law.

***American Law Reports* (A.L.R.)** American Law Reports collects and summarizes cases that relate to a particular topic or issue. A.L.R. Fed. and A.L.R. Fed. 2d collect and summarize cases that discuss federal issues, and A.L.R., A.L.R.2d, A.L.R.3d, A.L.R.4th, A.L.R.5th, and A.L.R.6th collect and summarize cases that discuss state law issues. A.L.R. is available in book form and on Lexis. com, LexisAdvance, Westlaw Classic, and WestlawNext.

Analogous Case An analogous case is a case that is similar to the client's case. An analogous case argument is an argument in which the attorney compares and contrasts the facts in an analogous case to the facts in the client's case or uses the reasoning from the analogous case to make an argument.

Annotated Codes An annotated code is a code that contains not only the text of the statutes but also historical notes, cross-references to other sources published by the same publisher, and Notes of Decisions or Case Notes. Thus, an annotated code is both a primary authority, because it sets out the law itself, and a finding tool because it can be used to find other primary authorities (cases that have interpreted and applied the statute) and secondary authorities (for example, practice books and treatises that discuss the statute).

Atlantic Reporter The *Atlantic Reporter* sets out the published decisions of the highest court and intermediate courts of appeals in the following states: Connecticut, Delaware, District of Columbia, Maine, Maryland, New Hampshire, New Jersey, Pennsylvania, Rhode Island, and Vermont. The decisions are organized by date and not by jurisdiction.

Attorney General Opinions The United States Attorney General is the attorney for the federal government's executive branch, and a state attorney general is the attorney for the executive branch of that state's government. Some of the opinion letters that attorneys general write answering their clients' questions are made available to the public in the form of attorney general opinions. The opinions that are made available to the public are persuasive authority and are usually available in both book and electronic formats.

BCite BCite the citatory that is on Bloomberg Law.

Black's Legal Dictionary *Black's Legal Dictionary* is a popular legal dictionary that is available in hardbound form, in paperback form, and on Westlaw Classic and WestlawNext™.

Bloomberg Law Bloomberg Law is a fee-based, computer-assisted research service.

The Bluebook: A Uniform System of Citation Because *The Bluebook* was written for law reviews, most of the text and examples describe how to cite material in footnotes. There is, however, a section — the blue pages — that describes how to modify the rules and examples for citations in memos and briefs.

Boolean Searching Boolean searches are named after George Boole, the British mathematician who developed the set of "connectors" that carry his name and that describe the logical relationships among search terms. When you do a Boolean — or "terms and connectors" — search, you search for documents using search terms and "connectors" that describe the relationship between terms. Some of the more common connectors are "and," which retrieves only those documents that contain both search terms; "or," which retrieves documents that contain at least one of the search terms; "but not," which retrieves documents that contain the first search term but not the second search term; "/s," which retrieves documents that contain both search terms in the same sentence; and "/50," which retrieves documents in which the search terms are within 50 words of each other (articles and conjunctions may not be counted). Because the connectors may vary from service to service, check the services' documentation to see which connectors are available and what they mean.

Briefs A brief is a document submitted to the court by a party or interested individual in which the party or individual argues that the court should or should not take a particular action. Some briefs are now available online. For example, Lexis.com, Lexis Advance, Westlaw Classic, and WestlawNext have databases containing briefs.

Case Law Case law includes both those cases that set out the common law and those cases that interpret and apply enacted law.

Citation A typical legal citation identifies an authority and gives readers the information needed to locate that authority. In addition, many citations give readers information that they can use to determine how much weight to give to the authority. The two most frequently used citation manuals are the *ALWD Citation Manual* and *The Bluebook: A Uniform System of Citation*. In addition, many states and courts have their own citation manuals or rules.

Citators Citators serve two purposes. First, they are used to determine whether a particular authority — for example a case — is still good law. Second, they are used to find other authorities that have cited to a particular case, statute, regulation, law review article, or other authority. Today, the two most commonly used citators are KeyCite®, which is available on Westlaw Classic and WestlawNext and *Shepard's*®, which is available on Lexis.com and LexisAdvance. Bloomberg Law also has a citator: BCite.

Code A code sets out statutes and regulations not in the order in which they were enacted, but by topic. Thus, in a code, all of the statutes or regulations relating to a particular topic are placed under a single title. For instance, in the *United States Code*, all of the federal statutes relating to interstate highways are placed under one title, all of the statutes relating to veterans' benefits are placed under a different title, and all of the statutes relating to Social Security benefits are placed under yet a different title.

Code of Federal Regulations (C.F.R.) The *Code of Federal Regulations* contains federal regulations currently in effect. These regulations are set out by topic and not in the order in which they were promulgated. For example, all of the federal regulations relating to income tax are set out under one title, and all of the federal regulations relating to the Americans with Disabilities Act are set out under another title. The Code of Federal Regulations is published in book form and is available on both free Internet sites and on fee-based websites like Lexis.com, LexisAdvance, Westlaw Classic, and WestlawNext.

Common Law The common law is a system of law that is derived from judges' decisions rather than statutes or constitutions.

Compiled Legislative Histories A compiled legislative history is a legislative history that has been compiled by an individual, an organization, or a service. Some of the best sources for compiled legislative histories are *United States Code and Administrative News* (U.S.C.A.A.N.) (in book form and on Westlaw Classic and WestlawNext); Nancy Johnson, *Sources of Compiled Legislative Histories* (2007); *Union List of Legislative Histories, Seventh Edition* (2002) (see www.llsdc.org/sourcebook/about-union-histories.htm); and the Lexis.com, LexisAdvance, Westlaw Classic, and WestlawNext legislative histories databases.

Congressional Record The *Congressional Record* is the official record of the proceedings and debates of the United States Congress and is available both in print and electronically. In print, the daily version is published at the end of each day that Congress is in session, and the multi-volume version is published at the end of each Congressional session. One of the best online sources is www.gpoaccess.gov/crecord/index.html. Its databases are updated daily, and, at the back of each daily issue, is the "Daily Digest," which summarizes the day's floor and committee activities.

Corpus Juris Secundum (C.J.S.) *Corpus Juris Secundum* (C.J.S.) is a multi-volume legal encyclopedia that is available both as a book and on Lexis. com, LexisAdvance, Westlaw Classic, and WestlawNext. Like Am. Jur., C.J.S. has more than four hundred articles, covering a wide range of legal topics set out in alphabetical order. C.J.S. is not jurisdiction specific: Instead of setting out federal law or a particular state's law, it discusses the law in general terms. Most attorneys use C.J.S. as a finding tool to obtain an overview of an area of law. C.J.S. uses West's Key Number System®.

Digests Digests are a finding tool used to locate cases. Each digest contains a number of topics, for example, criminal law, evidence, and real estate. Under each of these topics are a series of subtopics, and under the subtopics are annotations describing cases that have discussed those subtopics. Most states have state digests, which list cases from that state, and West, a Thomson Reuters business, publishes a series of regional digests and federal digests. Most digests also have descriptive word indexes and other finding aids.

Enacted Law Enacted law is a system of law created by the legislative branch. For example, statutes are enacted law.

Federal Civil Rules Handbook The *Federal Civil Rules Handbook* sets out the text of each Federal Rule of Civil Procedure; the authors' commentary, which includes a description of the rule; and citations to key cases.

Federal Legislative Histories Federal legislative histories contain some or all of the documents that were created during the process of enacting or amending a federal statute. For example, a federal legislative history might contain the text of the bill as it was originally submitted, transcripts from committee hearings, committee reports, and transcripts from any floor debates. While some judges use legislative histories as a tool for determining what Congress intended when it enacted or amended a particular statute, other judges give such histories little weight. As a legal researcher, look first for a compiled legislative history.

Federal Practice and Procedure *Federal Practice and Procedure* is a multi-volume treatise that sets out and discusses in detail the Federal Rules of Civil Procedure, the Federal Rules of Criminal Procedure, the Federal Rules of Evidence, and other federal rules.

Federal Register The *Federal Register* publishes copies of proposed federal regulations, copies of proposed changes to existing federal regulations, and the final version of the regulations that are ultimately promulgated. In addition, the *Federal Register* also publishes notices of hearings, responses to public comments on proposed regulations, and helpful tables and indexes. It is published almost every weekday, with continuous pagination throughout the year. Because the *Federal Register* uses continuous pagination, page numbers in the thousands are common. An online version of the *Federal Register* is available on the FDsys website (www.gpo.gov/fdsys/) and on Lexis.com, Lexis Advance, Westlaw Classic, and WestlawNext.

Federal Reporter; Federal Reporter, Second Series; Federal Reporter, Third Series The decisions of the United States Courts of Appeals are published in the *Federal Reporter* (F.), *Federal Reporter, Second Series* (F.2d), and *Federal Reporter, Third Series* (F.3d). The *Federal Reporter* has decisions from 1889 to

1924; the *Federal Reporter, Second Series*, has decisions from 1924 to 1993; and the *Federal Reporter, Third Series*, has decisions since 1993. Decisions are set out in chronological order and not by topic or by circuit.

Federal Rules of Evidence Manual The *Federal Rules of Evidence Manual* is a multi-volume treatise that sets out the text of each federal rule of evidence along with commentary and an annotated list of cases.

Federal Supplement; Federal Supplement, Second Series While most United States District Court decisions are not published, some are published in *Federal Supplement*; (F. Supp.) *Federal Supplement, Second Series*; (F. Supp. 2d) or in another specialized reporter, for example *Federal Rules Decisions* or *Bankruptcy Reporter*. The *Federal Supplement* has decisions from 1932 to 1998, and the *Federal Supplement, Second Series*, has decisions from to 1998 to the present.

Finding Tools Finding tools are what the name suggests: They are tools that help you locate primary and secondary authority. Some examples of finding tools are digests, annotated codes, and search engines. While digests serve only as finding tools, annotated codes contain both the primary authority (the statutes) and finding tools (Notes of Decisions or Case Notes, which are one-paragraph summaries of a point of law set out in a case, and cross-references to other primary and secondary authorities).

FindLaw.com FindLaw.com is a website sponsored by West, a Thomson Reuters business, that either sets out or has links to the electronic version of federal and state statutes and regulations, selected cases, court rules, and other legal materials.

Google™ Google is one of several search engines that can be used to locate websites on the Internet

Google™ Scholar Google Scholar is a searchable database that provides free access to the text of federal and state court opinions. To access Google Scholar, go to www.google.com and click on "More" and then on "Even more."

Headnotes A headnote is a one-sentence summary of a rule of law found at the beginning of a court's opinion. Because headnotes are written by the company publishing the reporter in which the opinion appears and not by the court, headnotes cannot be cited as authority.

Hornbooks Hornbooks are books written for law students that summarize an area of law and provide citations to key constitutional provisions, statutes, cases, and regulations. Legal researchers use hornbooks to obtain an overview of particular areas of law or issues.

Jump Cite A jump, or pinpoint, cite gives the specific page on which a particular quote, rule, or statement appears.

KeyCite® KeyCite is West's cite checking system. You can use it to determine if a case, statute, or regulation is still good law and to find other authorities that have cited to that case, statute, or regulation.

Key Number Key Numbers are part of West's Key Number System®. West has divided the law into more than four hundred topics. Under these topics, each point of law is assigned a Key Number. Once you identify the topic and

Key Number for a particular point of law, you can use that topic and Key Number to locate information related to that point of law in almost all of West's publications. For example, you can use the topic and Key Number to locate information in C.J.S.; in West's state, regional, and general digests; in secondary sources published by West; and on Westlaw Classic and WestlawNext.

Law Reviews and Journals Law reviews and journals are periodicals that contain articles written by law school professors, law students, judges, and attorneys. Law reviews and journals published by law schools are edited by students: Second- and third-year law students select and edit the articles that are published in these journals. Law reviews and journals published by other groups are usually edited by members of that group. For instance, the journal *Legal Writing* is edited by law school professors who teach legal writing.

Legislative History Legislative histories are a tool that attorneys and courts use to determine what Congress or a state legislature intended when it enacted a particular statute. In general, a legislative history consists of the original and amended texts of the bills, transcripts of committee hearings, committee reports, and transcripts of floor debates.

Lexis.com Lexis.com is LexisNexis's older fee-based service. It is being replaced with Lexis Advance.

Looseleaf Services Historically, looseleaf services were what their name suggests: a service that provided information in "looseleaf" notebooks, which were updated by removing outdated pages and replacing them with new pages. Today, most looseleaf services are available both in book form and on fee-based services like Lexis.com, Lexis Advance, Westlaw Classic, and WestlawNext Although each looseleaf service is different, most deal with specialized areas of law. For example, there are looseleaf services that deal with federal tax issues, with federal benefits issues (for example, Social Security), and with many other federal issues (for example, environmental issues). Most loose-leaf services provide a wide range of up-to-date information about these specialized areas. For instance, many of them set out the text of the applicable statutes and regulations, the text of proposed legislation and regulations, and summaries of relevant court and administrative decisions.

Mandatory Authority Mandatory authority is law that is binding on the court deciding the case: The court must apply that law. In contrast, persuasive authority is law that is not binding. Although the court may look to that law for guidance, it need not apply it. Determining whether a particular statute or case is mandatory or persuasive authority is a two-step process. You must first determine which jurisdiction's law applies (that is, whether federal or state law applies and, if state law applies, which state's law); you must then determine which of that jurisdiction's statutes and cases are binding on the court that will be deciding the case.

Moore's Federal Practice *Moore's Federal Practice* is a multi-volume treatise that sets out and discusses in detail the Rules of Civil Procedure, the Rules of Criminal Procedure, and the United States Court of Appeals and Supreme Court rules.

Natural Language Searching Unlike Boolean or terms and connectors searches, which allow you to determine the logical relationships between your search terms, natural language searches use an algorithm that weighs each search term based on its "rareness" and on its proximity to other search terms. In addition, unlike Boolean searches, which list your results by date, natural language searches list your results based on "relevance" scores, which are part of the algorithm. Both Lexis Advance and WestlawNext™ use natural language searching.

New York Supplement The *New York Supplement* sets out the published decisions of the New York Court of Appeals. The decisions are set out in date order.

North Eastern Reporter The *North Eastern Reporter* sets out the published decisions of the highest court and intermediate courts of appeals in the following states: Illinois, Indiana, Massachusetts, and Ohio. The decisions are organized by date and not by jurisdiction.

North Western Reporter The *North Western Reporter* sets out the published decisions of the highest court and intermediate courts of appeals in the following states: Iowa, Michigan, Minnesota, Nebraska, South Dakota, and Wisconsin. The decisions are organized by date and not by jurisdiction.

Notes of Decisions A Note of Decision is a one-sentence summary of a point of law set out in a case. Because Notes of Decisions are written by the attorneys who work for West, a Thomson Reuter business, you cannot cite them as authority. Instead, you must read and cite the cases from which they were drawn.

Nutshells *Nutshells* are one-volume paperback books written for students that summarize an area of law. The books are written by an expert in the area of law and are published by West, a Thomson Reuter business.

Overruled A case is overruled when, in a different case, a court determines that, in an earlier decision, the court applied the wrong rule of law. In contrast, a decision is reversed when, in the same case, a higher court reverses the decision of a lower court.

Pacific Reporter The *Pacific Reporter* sets out the published decisions of the highest court and intermediate courts of appeals in the following states: Alaska, Arizona, California, Hawaii, Idaho, Kansas, Nevada, New Mexico, Oklahoma, Oregon, Utah, Washington, and Wyoming. The decisions are organized by date and not by jurisdiction.

Parallel Citation If a case is published in more than one reporter, the citation to that case may include references to more than one reporter. The first reference will be to the official reporter. Any other references are called parallel citations. For example, the United States Supreme Court's decision in *Terry v. Ohio* is published in three reporters: *United States Reports* (U.S.), *Supreme Court Reporter* (S. Ct.), and *Supreme Court Reporter, Lawyers' Edition Second* (L. Ed. 2d). The first reference is to the official reporter, and the second and third references are parallel cites to unofficial reporters.

Persuasive Authority Persuasive authorities are cases, statutes, regulations, and secondary authorities that a court may consider, but is not required to consider, in deciding a case.

Pinpoint Cite A pinpoint, or jump, cite gives the specific page on which a particular quote, rule, or statement appears.

Primary Authority Primary authority is the law. For example, constitutions, statutes, regulations, and cases are primary authorities. Some primary authorities are mandatory authority, and some are only persuasive authority. For example, while a decision of the California Supreme Court is always primary authority, the only courts that are bound by that decision are California state courts. Thus, California Supreme Court decisions are mandatory authority in California but only persuasive authority in other states.

Regulations Regulations are promulgated by the executive branch under authority granted to it by the legislative branch. Regulations are similar in form and substance to statutes and are usually compiled into codes. For example, regulations promulgated by federal agencies are compiled and published in the *Code of Federal Regulations*.

Reporters Reporters are sets of books that set out the published decisions of one or more courts in the order in which the decisions were issued. For example, *United States Reports* has the decisions of the United States Supreme Court set out in date order, the *Pacific Reporter* has decisions from the state courts in the Pacific region set out in date order, and *Nebraska Reports* has decisions of the Nebraska Supreme Court set out in date order.

Reversed A decision is reversed when, in the same case, a higher court reverses the decision of a lower court. In contrast, a case is overruled when, in a different case, a court determines that in an earlier decision the court applied the wrong rule of law.

Search Engine A search engine is an Internet site that allows you to search for and retrieve websites. Some examples of search engines are Google and Bing.

Secondary Authority A secondary authority is an authority that explains or comments on the law. For example, practice manuals, treatises, and law reviews are secondary authority. A court is never bound by a secondary authority.

Session Laws Session laws are the laws enacted during a particular legislative session arranged in date order. The federal session laws are set out in a set called *Statutes at Large*.

Shepardize When you *shepardize* a case, you cite check the case to determine whether it is still good law and to identify other authorities that have cited that case. This is a generic term for cite checking a case, and can be done using *Shepard's*, which is on Lexis.com and LexisAdvance; KeyCite, which is on Westlaw Classic and WestlawNext™; or BCite, which is on Bloomberg Law.

Shepard's *Shepard's* is a system for cite checking cases, statutes, regulations, and other sources. Although it is still available in book form, most attorneys now use the version that is on Lexis.com or LexisAdvance. You can use *Shepard's* to determine whether a case, statute, or regulation is still good law and to find other authorities that have cited to that case, statute, or regulation.

Slip Opinion The phrase "slip opinion" refers to the court's opinion in the form that it is initially released by the court. Slip opinions do not have volume numbers, page numbers, or editorial features, such as, headnotes.

South Eastern Reporter The *South Eastern Reporter* sets out the published decisions of the highest court and intermediate courts of appeals in the following states: Georgia, North Carolina, South Carolina, Virginia, and West Virginia. The decisions are organized by date and not by jurisdiction.

Southern Reporter The *Southern Reporter* sets out the published decisions of the highest court and intermediate courts of appeals in the following states: Alabama, Florida, Louisiana, and Mississippi. The decisions are organized by date and not by jurisdiction.

South Western Reporter The *South Western Reporter* sets out the published decisions of the highest court and intermediate courts of appeals in the following states: Arkansas, Kentucky, Missouri, Tennessee, and Texas. The decisions are organized by date and not by jurisdiction.

Statutes at Large *Statutes at Large* contains the session laws enacted by Congress during a particular Congressional session. You may use the *Statutes at Large* when doing a legislative history for a federal statute.

Unannotated Codes An unannotated code has the text of statutes currently in effect. It does not, however, have cross-references to other sources or Notes of Decisions/Case Notes describing cases that have discussed a particular statutory section.

United States Code (U.S.C.) The *United States Code* is the official source for United States statutes. Although the *United States Code* sets out the text of all of the federal statutes currently in effect and historical notes, it does not have cross-references to other sources or Notes of Decisions/Case Notes.

United States Code Annotated (U.S.C.A.) The *United States Code Annotated* is an unofficial version of the *United States Code* published by West, a Thomson Reuter business. In addition to setting out the current version of the federal statutes, the U.S.C.A. has historical notes, which summarize amendments; cross-references to other materials published by West; and Notes of Decisions, which describe cases that have interpreted and applied the statute. The U.S.C.A. is available in book form and on Westlaw Classic and WestlawNext.

United States Code Congressional and Administrative News (U.S.C.C.A.N.) *United States Code Congressional and Administrative News* contains selected reprints and excerpts of committee reports, references to other reports, and references to the *Congressional Record*.

United States Code Service (U.S.C.S.) The *United States Code Service* is an unofficial version of the United States Code published by LexisNexis. In addition to setting out the current version of the federal statutes, the U.S.C.S. has historical notes, which summarize amendments; cross-references to other materials published by LexisNexis®; and case notes, which quote key language from cases that have interpreted and applied the statute. U.S.C.S. is available in book form and on Lexis.com and LexisAdvance.

Westlaw Classic Westlaw Classic is a fee-based, computer-assisted research service. It is being replaced by WestlawNext.

WestlawNext WestlawNext is a fee-based service for legal research that allows for "Google"-like searching: Users do not need to select a database or construct terms and connectors searches.

West's Key Number System® West's Key Number System® is a system developed by West, a Thomson Reuters business. Through the years, West has created a series of topics and within those topics, Key Numbers for each point of law. This set of topics and Key Numbers is West's Key Number System. When a court publishes an opinion, it sends a copy of its opinion to West, which assigns the case to an editor, who is an attorney. The editor identifies each point of law set out in the court opinion, writes a single sentence summarizing that point of law, and then assigns that summary a topic and Key Number. These summaries are used in two ways. First, West uses these summaries as headnotes for the case. In West publications, these headnotes are placed at the beginning of the case, after the name of the case but before the court's opinion. Second, these summaries are placed in the appropriate digests under their assigned topic and Key Number.

WEX Wex is a free legal dictionary and encyclopedia sponsored and hosted by the Legal Information Institute at the Cornell Law School. Wex entries are collaboratively created and edited by legal experts.

List of Reliable Websites

I. Constitutions
   - A. United States Constitution
     - www.law.cornell.edu/constitution/constitution.overview.html
     - http://supreme.justia.com/constitution/
     - www.findlaw.com/casecode/constitution/
   - B. State Constitutions
     - www.law.cornell.edu/statutes.html
     - http://law.justia.com/
     - Each state's official website
II. Statutes
   - A. United States Code
     - http://uscode.house.gov/
     - www.law.cornell.edu/uscode/
     - http://law.justia.com/us/codes/
   - B. State Codes
     - www.law.cornell.edu/states/listing.html
     - http://law.justia.com/
     - Each state's official website
   - C. Ordinances
     - http://statelocalgov.net/
     - http://municode.com/
     - County and city websites
III. Legislative Histories
   - A. Federal Legislative Histories
     - http://thomas.loc.gov/
     - www.gpo.gov/fdsys/

http://www.llsdc.org/sourcebook
http://lib.law.washington.edu/ref/fedlegishist.html

B. State Legislative Histories
www.law.indiana.edu/library/services/sta_leg.shtml
www.llrx.com/columns/reference34.htm
State-specific websites (using Bing or Google, search for the name of the state and the phrase "legislative history")

IV. Regulations

A. Code of Federal Regulations
www.gpo.gov/fdsys/browse/collectionCfr.action?collectionCode=CFR
www.law.cornell.edu/cfr/
http://law.justia.com/us/cfr/
Agency websites (for example, www.ssa.gov/regulations/)

B. State Regulations
http://law.justia.com/
Each state's official website

V. Cases

A. Federal Cases

1. United States Supreme Court
Google Scholar (http://scholar.google.com/schhp?hl=en&as_sdt=0,48)
www.supremecourtus.gov/opinions/opinions.html
http://supct.law.cornell.edu/supct/
http://supreme.justia.com/

2. United States Courts of Appeal, United States District Courts, and Specialized Courts
Google Scholar (http://scholar.google.com/schhp?hl=en&as_sdt=0,48)

B. State Cases
Google Scholar (http://scholar.google.com/schhp?hl=en&as_sdt=0,48)
State court websites

VI. Court rules

A. Federal
http://www.supremecourt.gov/ctrules/ctrules.aspx
http://www.law.cornell.edu/rules

B. State
www.llrx.com/courtrules/
Each state's court website

VII. Court filings and dockets
http://pacer.psc.uscourts.gov/

VIII. Government Officials, Public Records, Companies, People
www.firstgov.gov/
http://searchsystems.net/
www.sec.gov/edgar.shtml.
www.411.com/
www.dexonline.com

IX. Forms:
http://forms.lp.findlaw.com/
State Court websites

Index